# Fishermen in Wartime

A STEAM TRAWLER IN A GALE

# Fishermen in Wartime
## The Struggle at Sea During the First World War
## 1914-1918

Walter Wood

LEONAUR

*Fishermen in Wartime*
*The Struggle at Sea During the First World War 1914-1918*
by Walter Wood


First published under the title
*Fishermen in War Time*


Leonaur is an imprint of Oakpast Ltd

Copyright in this form © 2011 Oakpast Ltd


ISBN: 978-0-85706-747-0 (hardcover)
ISBN: 978-0-85706-748-7 (softcover)


**http://www.leonaur.com**

# Contents

# Preface

In the late Eighties I made my first trip to the North Sea fishing-grounds in a Grimsby smack, a beam-trawler which sailed and joined her fleet, working around Heligoland, at that time a British possession. For some days and nights we shot and hauled our gear within sight and quite easy reach of that freak island, with a handful of fisher-folk and lodging-house keepers as inhabitants—a lonely lump of land which jutted out of the sea and resembled the dismantled hull of a gigantic battleship. What I saw and heard then, thirty years ago, remains with undimmed clearness in my memory.

The fleeting system of fishing, as carried out by sailing smacks, had reached its zenith, and there were many signs of the revolution which the introduction of steam trawlers and drifters was to bring about in the fishing industry. When from my rough experiences of fishing off Heligoland I landed at Billingsgate from the carrier I made the old, old declaration that I had had enough of North Sea smacks and North Sea fishing-grounds to last my life-time; yet, as the warrior returns to the battlefield, so I went back to those hard fighting zones which produced the incomparable men who have done so much for the salvation of civilisation; and so that I might the more fully understand and sympathise with fishermen, I settled on the Yorkshire coast for five years.

From that time onward it was my good fortune to see trawlers and drifters at work in many regions—from the Shetlands southabout to the Bristol Channel; to watch them in the Atlantic, the Bay of Biscay, and off the Moroccan coast, and often to bear some sort of a hand in their labours; and during the long years that have passed since those depressing Grimsby days I have never lost touch with my friends of the North Sea and other fishing regions.

In story and historically I have tried to help the world to realise what the deep sea fishers in particular are and what they have done. Twelve years ago, in *The Enemy in Our Midst,* a title which has proved useful since to many writers and speakers, I told something of the horrors and devilries of a German invasion of England and of the part which North Sea fishermen played in the imaginary struggle; and in *North Sea Fishers and Fighters*, published long before the war broke out, I ventured on prophecies, which have been fulfilled, of what these men could do.

And so now, in giving this book to a public which has been magnanimously appreciative of courage and endurance in every form, I have special pride in feeling that I am doing at least something to make the fishermen's work and devotion more fully understood. In two cases the deep sea toilers speak for themselves—the repatriated skipper and "Submarine Billy." They related their experiences to me when I saw them on the East coast, and afterwards saw and approved of the typescripts of their narratives.

No man has a more profound admiration than I have for the mighty, all-protecting work of the British Navy, and I wish definitely to say that in seeming to neglect purely naval deeds I am merely carrying out the special task I have in mind, and that is to deal solely, and as completely as one may under the restrictions which so rightly exist, with the work of British fishermen in war-time.

CHAPTER 1

# The Raw Material

The Great War brought the fisherman, especially the toiler of the deep sea, into his own, and put him in the forefront of that mighty naval power on which, in the good providence of God, the safety not of England only but the whole civilised world depended. It saved him from obscurity and gave him that honoured place in public life from which for many generations he had been unjustly kept. Some such cataclysm as the war was needed to call adequate attention to the fisherman, for he was by nature incapable of singing his own praises or claiming his due.

There were few, even amongst those to whom the toilers of the deep had been a life-long study, who anticipated the vast development in the employment of the fisherman and his craft for purposes of war; naval authorities themselves were not able to forecast that growth, and to the world at large the extension of the fishers' operations was an almost incredible revelation.

The common view of fishing life was that if not so good it was, at any rate, not so bad, and there was reason for that general impression, for it was mostly based on observation made at romantic watering-places by holiday-makers who were susceptible to comforting impressions. There were the little brown-sailed craft beloved of the visitor, and the bluff, hearty fisherman, whose life apparently was made up of pleasant trips to sea, well within the protection of the land. There was the picturesque marketing of the catch, perhaps on a sun-bathed beach, followed by the return home, often to the little cottage under the hill or up the creek, which looked so snug and pretty.

There was perhaps the added attraction of the old, old story of the lover and his lass—he so big and strong and bronzed and handsome; she so comely and so much a daughter of the sea. All this delightful picture came into the view of the casual observer; an image seen largely through the artistic eye, and therefore to a great extent misleading, for that standpoint must ignore the sordid and unlovely.

That common view of fishing life was wholly wrong and incomplete. It was true that there were many little trips to sea on calm blue water, under glowing summer suns, and many safe havens to which the fisherman might run for shelter when the snarl of the rising wind was heard and the seething surge came up as herald of the growing sea. But the view left out of count the multitude of fishing-places on inhospitable coasts to which romantic visitors rarely went; and it did not include even a vague impression of the deep sea fishermen. Nor could it do so, for the poetic trifler at a Cornish haven probably had no knowledge of the Dogger, and had doubtless never heard of Grimsby, except to shudder and dismiss the sordid vision which the mention of the port aroused.

Visitors to a place like Scarborough could see something of the deep sea men, but rarely did the fashionable lady jeopardise her lovely dress or risk offending her dainty nose by going to look at the old town or the harbour where the fishing craft were moored. Yet from the Spa it all looked so romantic, especially on a moonlight night, with the soft summer breeze coming in from the sea, the Spa brilliantly illuminated, and the band playing delightful music. Here, again, the fishing element added to the picturesqueness and romance, and pretty heads were not troubled by thoughts of fishers who in winter gales had been dashed to death by monstrous seas on the deadly rocks on the Spa beach and on the very sea wall of the Spa itself.

That there were, on such a great extent of coast-line as the shores of Great Britain afforded, a very large number of men and boys engaged in fishing was obvious to the most unobservant seaside visitor, but of the fishers little was really known, and there was a general and profound ignorance of the lives of the deep sea men, especially those who ranked as "fleeters," and whose whole existence was practically spent on the Dogger and other banks, far from land and all the safety and comfort that it represents, exposed to every peril and torment of a notorious sea.

Wherever one went round the coast the same proof of immensity of raw material was evident, and it was fascinating and astonishing to see and study the various types of fisherman and fishing craft. For the secure waters of estuaries and almost landlocked bays there were little vessels which might have been built for pleasure purposes. In such a region as Morecambe Bay, on the Lancashire coast, there were the trim and graceful shrimpers, a complete contrast to the famous cobles on the shores of the great sister county Yorkshire, the Viking-like craft in which Grace Darling achieved renown, and which alone can work successfully such dangerous regions as Flamborough Head and the North and South Landings, and can make difficult harbours like Whitby.

There were the bigger shrimpers working the Thames Estuary, with headquarters at Leigh-on-Sea, and a cross between a coble and a smack, known as a "mule," which was well adapted for longer trips and heavier seas than the open cobles could contend with. From Land's End to John o'Groats, and up to the Orkneys and Shetlands, there were innumerable types of fishing craft, each particularly planned to do its special work, and the crews were almost as varied as the vessels.

The men who worked in some of the quiet Western waters were in not a few respects the opposites of the breed which shares the Flamborough headland with the sea-birds and sometimes, when the sea gives up its dead, finds a resting-place in the old churchyard. There many a fisherman has been buried, as quaint epitaphs show, amongst them that on William Brown, "who suffered in Bridlington Bay, 30th October, 1807," and John Thompson, also a fisherman, who was drowned on January 10, 1814:—

*From home he went with mind most free,*
*His livelihood to gain at sea;*
*He ne'er returned, a furious wave,*
*Cast him into a watery grave;*
*A grave in motion termed the deep.*
*Left child and widow for to weep.*

On the Eastern seaboard there were few grounds the fishing of which did not involve the constant peril of the North Sea, though on the Channel shores and Western coast there were localities in which these toilers had comparative immunity. But whatever the local circumstances might be, the spirit was the same, and undaunted courage and endurance in rescuing shipwrecked people was shown by fishermen, for they mostly manned the life-saving craft. During a very heavy gale in December, 1886, the Southport lifeboat was capsized in the attempt to rescue the crew of the *Mexico*, and all the crew except two men were drowned.

The St. Anne's lifeboat also capsized in the same gale, and of the two crews 27 members perished. That disaster occurred in a danger-ous region of sandbanks and channels, between the Mersey and the Ribble, a region which was fished by men whose havens might be looked upon, as safe and peaceful.

Apart from the heroic life-saving deeds of fishermen in lifeboats and other craft which left the shore, there were numberless achieve-ments on the deep sea by trawlermen who were working steam or sailing vessels. It might be a case like the German liner, *Elbe*, whose few survivors, after a terrible collision, were brought to Lowestoft by a North Sea smack, or some smaller vessel which had come to grief and whose crew or passengers were rescued by a fisher crew; or it might be one of the innumerable unrecorded instances of fishermen saving fishermen, and taking it as part of the day's work, neither expecting nor receiving acknowledgment or reward. It might be any one of these many cases of stress and peril in which the fishermen distin-guished themselves and maintained and developed that courage and tenacity which served civilisation so nobly in the time of extremity and sore need.

The raw material was abundant and was everywhere available around the British coast, and that material was to be taken and shaped into one of the most wonderful and efficient bodies that had ever been evolved.

No work of skilled craftsman, fashioned out of crude and shapeless clay, was more remarkable than the vast and disciplined army of mine-sweepers, patrollers and other adjuncts of the Navy, who were brought into being from the rough and ready and too much ignored com-munity whose home was the humble little fishing vessel, and whose constant workground was the stormy deep.

The war produced its many evolutions and revolutions, and out-standing amongst even the most striking of them all was the change amongst the fishermen. Women turned to bus conducting, tram-driving, motor and van driving, postman's work, farm labouring, and perilous munition tasks; gently nurtured girls forgot their luxurious earlier days in the heavy demands of voluntary hospital work—all classes of men and women everywhere were being altered out of rec-ognition; but there was no change more astonishing than that of the unpromising fisherman who had turned smart naval seaman, or the grim skipper who had sported a battered bowler, an intensely fishy dopper, and enormous dumpers, who had gravitated when travelling to the crowded third-class smoker, turned gold-braided, blue-clad

Chief Skipper or Skipper, with a place in the *Navy List* and the *Gazette*, and a first-class pass when travelling by train.

The raw material could be divided into two great classes, the inshore fishers and the deep sea men; the former working in open boats near the land and the latter going to the North Sea grounds and much farther afield in sailing and steam vessels that were admittedly the finest seaboats of their class in the world.

The inshore fishers were the remote successors of the wild races in ancient Britain who in their primitive canoes and coracles fished the estuaries, lakes and rivers, and in course of time went seaward in stouter craft. When war broke out there were still to be found, in Western waters, people who employed the coracle in pretty much the same shape and way as the ancient Briton, and there were, at various places remote from railway stations, methods of conveyance of fish in use which were almost as primitive as the coracles. A woman's head would support a basket of fish, or a donkey's panniers be filled; and woman and beast would have a long, rough journey to make before the selling-place of the fish was reached. The woman took this burden bearing as much a matter of course as the donkey did, for both had been born to it. In a princely place like Edinburgh the quaint old fish-wives could be seen, crowned with great loads; and at Flamborough Head, far from a railway station, the patient ass climbed the rocky pathways with his panniers.

The inshore fishers carried on their calling in a way that differed altogether from the methods of the deep sea men. They were essentially home-birds, making short trips to sea, trips of seldom more than a few hours' duration, day or night, and always with a good prospect of getting back to port in case of bad weather. But the deep sea man's home was his sailing smack or steam trawler, and many perils and sufferings were stolidly endured by toilers in the days when smacks went fleeting. They sailed from Grimsby, Hull, Scarborough, Whitby, Boston, Ramsgate, Yarmouth and Lowestoft to the North Sea grounds; while the English Channel was worked by Brixham and neighbouring smacks.

In 1887, when the smacks had reached their fullest development, two large fleets and three small fleets worked from Hull, frequenting the Dogger all the year round, the number of hands employed varying from 2,200 in summer to 2,900 in winter. Two large and several small fleets from Grimsby, with about 2,750 hands, worked between Heligoland and the Sylt in summer and on the Dogger in winter;

while many other smacks consistently worked off the Texel and the Dutch coast.

Many a quaint old smacksman's yarn related to adventures ashore at Heligoland and on the Dutch coast, for when calms prevailed and the island and the coast were handy, it was no hard thing to get ashore in the boat. Extensive consumption of very cheap and very deadly foreign spirits was an almost inevitable episode in these shore visits, and some of the most terrible of the contemporary North Sea tragedies were due to this indulgence in raw and fiery drink.

There were available at the beginning of the war, for naval purposes, not a few of the old school of skipper and man who had a thorough knowledge of the Heligoland and neighbouring waters; to whom the secrets of the banks in the dangerous shallow depths were readily revealed by the lead, and who had a wondrous instinct for telling the turn and run of a tide. This special knowledge proved inestimably useful.

The ancient reputation of the Yarmouth men as fishers was maintained when the smacks were supreme, for the port sent four fleets to sea, including the famous Short Blue. Three fleets fished between Terschelling and Heligoland; the East Dogger was worked and the grounds between Schouwen and the Texel. That was in the summer, when the number of hands employed was about 2,880; in winter, when the number of hands was reduced to about 2,000, the Short Blues would work at the east end of the celebrated Silver Pits; the Leleu and Columbia fleets would trawl the Botney Gut, and the Knoll fleet would be herring catching.

These old fleets were composed of smacks which went out for an eight weeks' or longer voyage, the catches of fish being "ferried" in the smacks' boats to the attendant steam carrier, which kept up communication with London and other markets. This ferrying was perilous work in bad weather and the fleets often suffered heavy loss in life through the deeply-laden boats being capsized or swamped. There was little or no chance for the fisherman, who as a rule could not swim, and wore heavy clothes and very heavy boots, some of the latter reaching to the hip. In this matter of boarding the trawlerman was largely a fatalist and was accustomed to declare that fishermen were used to being drowned.

There was no industrial class of which so little was known and in which therefore so little interest was taken, as the deep sea fishermen. The very docks from which they sailed were unfathomed mysteries to the majority of the public, the vessels were known only vaguely as pretty or picturesque fishing smacks, and the men, if seen at all, were reckoned quite as romantic in their way as the Venetian boatman or the Portuguese who took the tourist up the Douro. So at least would the Spa lounger think, while watching the brown-sailed smack heaving on the blue swell, slowly disappearing, going, presumably, for a pleasant night's fishing; but as a matter of fact beginning a two months' voyage of monotonous toil and eating and drinking, making the best of a poor existence.

In the small, dirty, dark hole which did duty in even the finest smacks as a cabin, men slept and ate and drank unbrokenly from day to day and week to week, the only preparation for bed being taking off boots and head-dress, though frequently the boots were left on.

Fully dressed, utterly exhausted, the fisherman climbed into the stifling black box he called a bunk, drew the shutter, and in an atmosphere which would suffocate an ordinary person sought forgetfulness in sleep; or he would just stretch himself on the locker or the sodden greasy floor and know nothing till the unwelcome roar of a voice came down the tiny hatchway, "Haul up your trawl, boys, haul!" And so, as likely as not, especially in the bitter winter, with torn and bleeding hands that never had the chance to heal, the laborious work of getting the trawl up, cleaning, packing and ferrying the fish, would be done.

At the end of such a life a man might be a smack-owning skipper; sometimes he was, but more often he found a haven in the workhouse. There were such men who, having gone first to sea as miserable little apprentices, could look back on half-a-century and more afloat, and say that in each of those fifty years there had not been more than five or six full weeks ashore. It was an inhuman, soulless existence, fit companion to the slaves of the pit and the factory, survivals of the "good old times" which, when the truth was known about them, were so abominably bad, except in the cases of the favoured few.

One most important individual was present with every sailing or steam fleet, and that was the thoroughly experienced skipper who, because of his wide knowledge of fishes and the fishing areas, was appointed to the direction of an assemblage of vessels and bore the title of Admiral of the Fleet. He had control of his fleet, and at his bidding fifty sail or forty steam—more or less as the case might be—would leave one ground and make for another; in obedience to his signals trawls would be shot or hauled, fish would be boarded, or, if bad weather prevailed, the boats would not be launched—but it had to be very bad weather indeed for the admiral to refuse to allow the men to ferry the fish to the carrier.

The Admiral of the Fleet had a vice-admiral, as wise and experienced as himself, to take command in his absence or indisposition. This arrangement proved of very great value when the fishermen were absorbed as naval ratings, for they had the advantage of having worked according to a system and under discipline; and the training in this respect proved particularly valuable to the fishermen who became sweepers, and worked in flotillas.

Some of these admirals and vice-admirals could claim forty or fifty years' experience at sea—and let it be remembered that with the exception of a very few weeks ashore in the course of a year the whole of that long period was spent on the wild North Sea waters, far from land, in little ships which had to ride out any storm that raged. No country in the world except England could point to exactly the same type of man or vessel, though the French and Newfoundlanders had some experienced and gallant fellows toiling on the Atlantic fishing-banks and in the inhospitable Icelandic regions. Dr. W. T. Grenfell had done much to show the world what the Newfoundland codmen were—the men who rallied to their Motherland and did such noble service at sea and on, the Western Front; and Pierre Loti, in his powerful story *Le Pêcheur d'Islande*, dealt with the hard life of the fishers of Brittany who went far north to reap the harvest of the sea.

Hard men, too, and schooled in discomfort, were the engineers and firemen of the trawlers and the drifters; men of whom countless deeds of heroism and endurance were to be recorded in official archives but not made known in public. In some of the fine and big modern fishing vessels there were corresponding engine-rooms, but there were many engine-rooms in which in hot or bad weather the staff had persistently uncomfortable times, when heavy rolls and pitches made the very body ache in the attempts to keep a footing and to escape being hurled into the moving machinery or against the red-hot furnace. Battened down in a steam trawler, whose notorious sea-shipping propensities earned for her the title of a "washer," the little engine-room staff had the added misery of poisoned air to breathe.

This engine-room life was mercilessly wearing and tormenting, and only necessity enabled human beings to live it; but it was the very sternness of the existence which enabled the men trained in that school to bear and survive the hardships and dangers of the sweeping

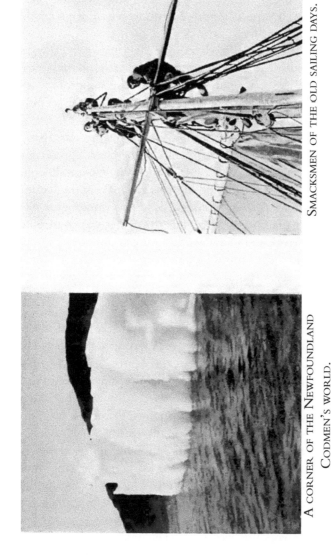

SMACKSMEN OF THE OLD SAILING DAYS.

A CORNER OF THE NEWFOUNDLAND
CODMEN'S WORLD.

and patrolling which they subsequently undertook.

So that the wonderful work of the mine-sweepers and fishermen and many of the patrollers may be understood it is necessary to describe the vessels in which that work was done, especially at the beginning of the war, when the craft actually employed in fishing were taken over for use by the naval authorities and there had not been time to produce the special improvements which subsequently helped the fishermen so greatly in various ways.

The principal fishing vessels were divided into two classes, steam trawlers and steam drifters, leaving out of account the swarms of smaller vessels like sailing smacks, sailing drifters, motor vessels and half-decked and open boats. For the purposes of this explanation steam trawlers and steam drifters only need attention.

The steam trawler, like the steam drifter, stood in a class apart. Each was built for a special purpose, and though there was a great similarity between them they were in several important respects different, for the trawler would regularly go long voyages, making the Iceland and White Sea trips as a matter of course, as well as working the deep sea grounds nearer the home ports; while the drifter was constructed for less strenuous work and in waters that were seldom more than a few hours' run from those ports. The trawler worked with the huge trawl, scooping up every sort of fish, shooting her gear and towing it; while the drifter, specially built for the herring fishery, shot her nets and then rode, or drifted, with them, at the will of wind and tide.

The steam trawler was the remarkably successful development of the old paddle-boats which were experimentally fitted with the beam-trawl for fishing purposes in the North Sea, and began that revolution which in a few years doomed the sailing fleets. The huge, cumbersome beam-trawl, which involved so much laborious work, especially in the days of sheer man-handling, before the helpful steam capstan was provided, was fitted in the quaint squat paddle-boats which had already done a life's work in towing and "seeking" on the North Sea—towing being the arranged work, and "seeking" the more precarious, but also more exciting, employment of scouring the seas, especially after a gale, in the hope of picking up a lame duck or some other salvage job or pilotage.

No pioneer work was ever undertaken without some pessimist predicting speedy and humiliating failure; and there were those who with gloomy joy foretold the downfall of the first steam trawlers. But to the croakers' confusion these experimental vessels were a prompt and sure success, and to the far-seeing it was clear that they had come to stay and be forerunners of an enormous fleet of steam fishing craft.

The time soon came when the paddle-boats were laid aside and the screw vessel alone was built for fishing work, some of the most notable of these craft being the strong, seaworthy steam carriers, or "cutters," which ran between the fishing fleets and Billingsgate, from the grounds off Heligoland, the Dogger, and elsewhere, to London River and back, scorning storms, making their appointed runs with almost train-like regularity, and keeping fit and busy the fine, brave, powerful men whose lives were given up entirely to this perilous and heavy work.

These steam carriers—successors to the actual sailing "cutters" which in earlier days had maintained communication between the fleets and the markets—were equipped with trawling gear, so that a vessel reaching a fleet in good time could make a shot or two before her turn came to take on board the fish which had been caught by the sailing smacks composing the fleet. The carriers were in their prime in the late eighties, and famous amongst them were the *Pelican, Gannet, Cormorant, Albatross*, and *Flamingo*. The *Pelican* was a Hull-built vessel, of iron, launched in 1884, 133ft. 5in. long, 21ft. 7in. broad, 11ft, deep, with a net tonnage of 141 and a gross of 244, and engines of 68 horse-power nominal. The *Flamingo*, built at Hull in the following year, was somewhat larger; but these five vessels were sisters, and amongst them ran enormous distances, did a vast amount of work and weathered many heavy gales and thudded through many a deadly fog before their day was done and they gave place to bigger and finer carriers.

The trawling industry had reached a state of high development before the steamboat came and pronounced the doom of the smack. Brixham and one or two more old-time ports on the Channel seaboard were the first homes of the trawler, which came into being, as a small vessel of a round score tons, in the middle of the eighteenth century. From Plymouth the trawlers would go to sea in the morning, fish during the day and return to port in the evening, and in those fine sheltered waters in the good weather the life could not have been unenjoyable. The Brixham men made longer trips, sailing on the Monday morning, returning with their fish on the following morning and going to sea again in the same way until the welcome Saturday ended a week's work.

In these handy little seaworthy craft some fine fishing was done by the Brixham men and their neighbours, though the number of vessels and crews was not large. That number gradually grew, and in 1872 about 100 smacks were registered at Brixham.

The fame of the North Sea as a fishing-ground extended, and wise men went East, settling first at Barking, whence many a stout smack sailed past the Nore to the trawling banks, and at last it became obvious that Grimsby was destined to be the greatest fishing centre. That port, indeed, developed with phenomenal rapidity. In 1790 the population was under 1,000; but in 1916 the number was nearly 75,000, and of these people the majority subsisted on the fisheries. In the hey-day of the smacks, when the sailing trawler had become a vessel of considerable proportions and carried a crew of five, Grimsby alone had nearly 900 of these craft; but not one remained when steam had got the mastery, and a vessel which had cost £1,600 to build and equip fetched only a few pounds. Five splendid smacks, for instance, which had cost about £7,000 to build and fit out, realised a total of only £215. When Grimsby became the largest fishing port in the world an enormous fleet of steam trawlers was registered there.

Some of these modern fishing vessels were uncommonly fine and powerful, especially those which made the long voyages such as Iceland and the White Sea. A steam trawler reached a length of 150ft., and when fully laden with coal, ice and stores, and starting for fishing-grounds a thousand miles or more away, she would carry about 250 tons. The gigantic growth of the steam fishing industry is shown by the simple statement that while in 1886 there were practically no steam trawlers in existence, in twenty years there were no fewer than 2,400 at work, most of these being attached to Grimsby, Hull and Aberdeen. In 1906 the quantity of fish landed from trawlers and line fishing vessels was 677,937 tons, valued at £8,726,508.

Vast numbers of steam drifters, too, had come into existence, superseding the sailing craft, though there were still great numbers of these fine vessels employed, just as there were still considerable numbers of sailing smacks, equipped with the beam-trawl, at work, leaving ports like Brixham, Ramsgate and Lowestoft. These sailing trawlers made short trips, rarely extending over a week, and less if the catches warranted an earlier return to port.

A typical steam trawler, built in 1916, was 117ft. long, 22½ft. broad, and 13½ft. deep, bunker capacity about 125 tons; with triple expansion engines, 75 nominal horse-power boiler, with a working pressure of 180lb., and a large double-barrelled winch of 1,000 fathoms capacity. Her Admiralty hire rate was more than £132 a month. She was offered for sale, was described as a "really magnificent boat, built to a special specification and fitted with all the very latest improvements." The price asked for her was £11,750, a sum which was about twice as large as the cost of such a vessel before the war. A pair of steam trawlers, sister boats, one built in 1912 and the other in 1913, were offered for sale at £22,600, for the two taken together; and for three fine steam trawlers offered in one lot the "owners' ideas" were £35,000 for the three taken together, but it was alluringly intimated that doubtless business could be done on the basis of a prompt offer of £32,500 for the three.

There were larger trawlers than those mentioned, and very many smaller; but these details will afford an understanding of the dimensions of the trawlers which were so extensively employed in connection with the Navy. From the ordinary standpoint they were almost grotesquely small; yet this was the sort of vessel which throughout the year withstood the heaviest North Sea gales and in which deep sea men would go, as they often did, to any part of the world. Trawlers built for the Colonies and Japan had been taken to those remote countries under their own steam and had completed their long voyages with perfect success, suffering neither damage to ship nor loss to crew.

It was significant of the immense development in the growth of the fishing industry throughout the world and of the steam trawler in particular, that builders were prepared to submit plans, specifications and prices for vessels which were considered suitable for special conditions of fishing anywhere, and to send "an experienced representative to confer with the authorities at any foreign or colonial port" at which it was desired to establish the fishing industry.

A modern yard would have accommodation for laying down a score or more steam trawlers or drifters, and before the war there were to be seen at important centres like Aberdeen a dozen fine trawlers on the stocks at one time, while at an inland town such as Selby a cluster of powerful boats was at any time visible, the peculiarity of this shipbuilding yard being that the trawlers were launched into the narrow river broadside on, making a fine crested wave as the vessel entered the water, and giving her the first of many shakings that she would have to endure in her stormy lifetime. Many splendid specimens of this form of fishing vessel were constructed at the Yorkshire town.

The steam drifter was an inevitable development of the sailing drifter, a type of craft with which the herring fishery had been prosecuted for a long period, and the direct successor of the boats which centuries before had carried on the herring fishery from the ancient port of Yarmouth.

The sailing herring drifter was a very famous vessel with two masts. Of these the foremast was so made as to lower backward into a "tabernacle," so that the fishing operations might be easier and generally helped. The mizenmast was fixed in the ordinary way. These drifters were fully-decked craft, with excellent use made of all the space both on deck and below. The average length was rather more than 50ft., with a beam of 17ft., and a depth of 7ft.—smaller ships than the trawling smack, but they were not expected to meet the same prolonged bad weather far from land. These drifters carried a crew of 10 or 12, and in addition to the considerable accommodation needed for them there were below compartments for the nets, warps and salt.

The steam drifter was in the first instance built mostly of wood, but gradually steel was employed and the size of the vessel grew considerably, until a fine drifter would have a length of about 100ft. and a speed of ten knots. Such a vessel would fetch a high price, and a craft built in 1898, of oak, 63ft. long, would command £750. For a wooden steam drifter built in 1900, 76ft. long, £2,650 was asked. A wooden steam drifter which eight years previously had changed hands at £950 was sold by public auction at Fraserburgh in the autumn of 1917 for £2,900.

There was little difference between the net which was used with the old beam-trawl and that which was employed with the otter gear. In the later and greatly improved method the use of the heavy and cumbersome beam was abandoned, and it was replaced by two boards which varied, according to the size of the vessel, from about 8ft. by 4ft. to 10ft. by 5ft. These boards, which weighed 7cwt. or 8cwt. each, were of very ingenious design and exceptional strength, qualities which well fitted them for the hard and strenuous work they had to do. They were so balanced that they moved forward on their longest edge, the result being that the mouth of the net was kept open to the fullest extent. Each board was secured and towed by a separate steel wire–warp of great strength, ranging from 600 to 1,200 fathoms in length—that is to say, a powerful steam trawler would have these warps up to a length of one and a-quarter statute miles.

These immense coils of steel wire needed the utmost skill and care in handling, but in spite of the exercise of both fatal and serious accidents in connection with the warps were common. It would

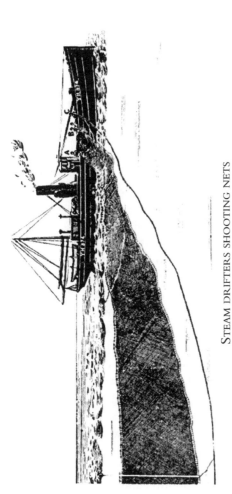

Steam drifters shooting nets

A steam trawler at work. The diagram shows the trawler-warps and the method of dragging the great net on the bottom of the sea

sometimes happen, especially in bad weather, that in the difficult and complicated operation of hauling the gear a wire-warp would tauten suddenly, and that a man who was inadvertently in the way would lose a limb—and indeed the terrible slash would at times sever a man in halves. These dreadful hazards were amongst the constant perils of the trawlerman's work at sea.

When a large drifter's "fleet" of herring-nets was successfully shot it formed a wall of netting in the sea which was more than two miles long and extended about 30ft. below the surface of the water. The successful handling of these nets required great experience and skill on the part of the skipper and his crew.

Side by side with the development of the fishing industry itself there had been a corresponding growth in the perfecting of vessels and appliances; and ships and gear had reached a stage of excellence which was singularly creditable to designers and constructors.

The methods of steam trawling and drifting which were in such wide and efficient employment before the war gave a thorough training of the skippers and fishermen who were called upon to apply them to the work of sweeping the seas clear of mines and to the task of netting or otherwise dealing with enemy submarines.

In addition to the two great classes of vessels which have been described, the steam trawlers and the steam drifters, there were enormous numbers of other vessels like the Scotch luggers and the craft which went long-lining from East coast, particularly Yorkshire, ports. These liners were very often old yawls whose crews, working from their small boats, ran great risks at sea in thick weather. They had a valuable knowledge of the North Sea and its many peculiarities.

The Scotch herring men were a race apart, for they were a combination of the crofter and the fisher, following the summer fishing down the East coast, where ports were densely packed with their shapely, handy vessels at the height of the herring season, when large numbers of Scotch "lasses" took an important share in the industry.

Just before the war broke out the herring fishery had begun and was in full progress in those northern regions where, so soon, the Grand Fleet was to take up its battle position and form the mightiest protection that had ever been afloat. At that period, somewhere in the northern mists, nearly a thousand steam drifters were assembled for the herring fishing, ready in due season to go south; but many of them went north and east and west as well, to play a great and gallant part in combating the craft and cruelty of German submarine commanders.

Such was the raw material in fishermen and fishing vessels which the country had the priceless benefit of commanding when the War was forced by Germany upon unwilling and unready peoples. The *personnel* was available on a vast scale; the *matériel* also was at hand, and because of the full and growing use which was made of both the Navy was largely helped in creating that colossal marine barrier which the most desperate and persistent efforts of the Germans could neither break nor weaken.

## CHAPTER 2

# The Call to Arms

When war broke out the British Navy put that grim grip on Germany which was never relaxed, but grew harder with the passing of the years. The whole colossal force of the fleet was brought to bear against the common enemy of man, and the German Navy, "willing to wound, and yet afraid to strike," was caged in Kiel, as impotent to fight as a toothless tiger is to bite. That the German Navy was powerless to give fair battle to the British was a painful truth to be perforce admitted by even the most rabid victim of *Kultur*. For all the good it seemed to do, the German Navy might as well have been on Lake Geneva or the Sunless Sea of Kubla Khan in Zanadu.

There was no hope of victory through fair fighting. Powerful though the German Navy was, skilful and courageous though some of the few honest fighters amongst the Germans were, at the beginning of the war, yet the overwhelming superiority of the British Navy made maritime supremacy for Germany hopeless, especially when added to Britain's naval might there was the sea strength of her Allies. But what the German could not hope to do in fair and open conflict he believed he could accomplish by adopting stealthy tactics, by throwing to the winds everything which stood for honour and humanity and resorting to methods of murder and outrage which made his name a by-word for all that was cowardly and infamous.

One of the very first of the German naval acts at sea, acts performed not by the German Navy, which could not leave its land-locked hiding-place, but by sporadic action of units let loose upon the waters, was to run amok at British steam trawlers which were peacefully fishing in the North Sea, sink and destroy the vessels, and take as many of the fishermen prisoners as they could capture. It was an unwarrantable and craven performance, worthy of the nation that in course of time was to sink the *Lusitania*, to raid defenceless ports and cities, and to force the whole civilised world to band together for the maintenance of justice and the defence of humanity.

Fervent hope was centred in the unlimited warfare of the U-boats, and early in the war vast faith was put in the mine. There was good reason for hoping that the effects of the mine on British sea-borne commerce would be paralysing, for the mines were so plentifully sown and in such wide areas, and the means of combating the danger were so apparently inadequate. But the poison produced the antidote, and no sooner was the extent of the peril realised by the British Admiralty than recourse was had to that raw material which has been described and there was the call to arms.

Some time before the war broke out there was in being the nucleus of the mine-sweeping fleet which speedily grew to such gigantic proportions. The naval authorities bought steam trawlers at Grimsby, Fleetwood and North Shields for mine-sweeping purposes, and steps were taken to organise a reserve fleet of 100 modern British steam trawlers for use in time of war. It was believed that the intention was that the reserve should consist of vessels belonging chiefly to the trawling fleets of Grimsby, Aberdeen and North Shields, because the crews of trawlers having those ports as headquarters were thoroughly acquainted with the East coast and the North Sea. There were, of course, other ports of the same description.

When those preliminary details were published it was understood that power would be obtained to call on a skipper for each vessel, who would doubtless receive a retaining fee, and also on about 1,000 of the members of the trawlers' crews. It was further expected that the trawlers secured by the authorities would be reconstructed in accordance with the Admiralty's special requirements; their speed in particular being increased, and special trawling apparatus and gear being fitted; and that the crews would undergo a period of special training each year, lasting probably from ten to twenty days.

At that time the Admiralty ordered their recently acquired steam trawlers, *Osprey II.* and *Josephine I.*, of Fleetwood; *Assyrian*, of Grimsby, and *Nunthorpe Hall*, of North Shields, which were then acting as tenders to the torpedo school-ship *Actæon*, at Sheerness, to be renamed *Seaflower*, *Sparrow*, *Spider* and *Seamew*. In the official descriptions these vessels, when actually added to the Navy, were described as of 550 and 500 tons and 400 indicated horse-power, which made them look much more formidable than the system of calculating tonnage and horse-power prevailing in relation to fishing vessels.

This nucleus was soon enlarged; more vessels of the same type were acquired and added to the Navy, being originally described as "miners," and numbered, and afterwards called Special Service Vessels. Later, however, when the nucleus had grown to a fleet, a definite list of "trawlers commissioned" was published, and this showed that in the middle of August, 1914, there were 107 of these vessels in commission. In addition to these craft there were eight obsolete torpedo-gunboats—the *Circe, Jason, Speedy, Leda, Gossamer, Speedwell, Seagull* and *Skipjack,* which were specially fitted out for mine-sweeping purposes, as well as other vessels as need arose and experience dictated. Amongst the minelayers were three vessels of about 2,000 tons each, and of high speed, which had capacity for 400 naval mines in two cases and 300 in the other.

In the earliest stages of the war the mine-sweeping fleet was manned by the Trawler Section, consisting at that time of some 140 skippers and 1,100 men; but this was the mere skeleton of the gigantic force which came into being. Admiral Jellicoe, at the beginning of 1917, publicly made known that nearly 2,500 skippers were then employed as Skippers, R.N.R., and it had been previously stated that 100,000 fishermen were serving with the Navy; in fact, two and a half years after the war began three-quarters of the first-class fishing vessels were on Admiralty service, and the great majority of the fishermen had joined the Navy.

This magnificent result was the fishers' answer to the call to arms. It is true that compulsion had come into operation; but no force had been necessary to get the sweepers and patrollers into the Navy. The country had called, and as the fishermen and coasting men had hurried in their little craft to meet and fight the Invincible Armada, so the inshore fisher and the deep sea men in their little drifters and steam trawlers rose in their thousands to crush the barbarous enemy.

The galleons of Spain were bearing proudly down upon England to put a free people under an abominable bondage; the battleships of Germany were waiting for the chance to get supremacy at sea and enable a crushing swoop to be made in the very midst of the people who were Germany's most dangerous, most powerful, and most bitterly hated rivals. Spanish prisoners, when the Most Happy Armada had been shattered by English guns and storms at sea—"*God blew with His wind, and they were scattered,*" said Elizabeth, on a medal which was struck—plainly told what the Spanish purpose was. The captain of

*Our Lady of the Rosary*, which came from Ribadeo, in Galicia, admitted that the landing was to be in London River; "and it was resolved by the whole company that in what place soever they should enter within the land, to sack the same, either city, town, village, or whatsoever. . . . They were determined to put all to the sword that should resist them." To these terrors a greater was to be added, for "the King of Spain would establish the Inquisition in this realm."

But the *dons* of Spain fell before the English sea-dogs like the autumn leaves in Vallombrosa; the castle-like galleons were battered and beaten by the handy little English craft—of the thirty-four Queen's ships eight were of less than 100 tons, three being of fifty, and one, the *Cygnet*, of thirty only, with twenty men and three guns.

The parallel holds good with regard to Germany. Germans were to win, and were then to impose their "frightfulness" on the English and other peoples What that "frightfulness" meant was but too terribly shown in the case of Belgium, a country which had been sacrificed to the necessity that knew neither law nor honour.

The little ships from the coast, largely manned by fishermen, had helped to save England from the despotic *don*; they had helped to fling him back into the sea on which he had dared to set forth on his sinister adventure; and little ships of Great Britain, whose crews also were fishermen, shared in crushing, at the very outset, the criminal intentions of the modern Huns.

Centuries before the Armada enterprise there had come to the East coast of England, from Jutland and the neighbouring islands, the barbarians who were called Goths, predecessors of the modern Huns, and they found the East coast so much to their liking that they settled there as much as they were allowed to do. Their successors would fain have done likewise; but the English people would have none of them; and that was the message which was given to them when British fishermen answered the call to arms and rallied to the service of their country under the White Ensign.

When the Armada came, when England was in peril, the fiery signal flashed throughout the land. In response to it the mariners of all sorts gathered in their might, and from that hour the Spanish enterprise was doomed. So when the challenge for world supremacy was flung to the world and was taken up unhesitatingly by Great Britain, with other defenders of right and freedom; when the Germans at the outset sowed their deadly mines broadcast, the skilled, brave men of the deep sea rallied to their country's call. They put at their country's service that priceless knowledge which they had gained from life-long toil on fishing-banks, working their drifting or trawling gear, sweeping up the fish as, later, they were to sweep up the far-scattered mines of Germany. In doing that they helped largely towards the preservation of the Navy and the merchant shipping, on which the food supply of the British people depended and without which it would not have been possible to perform the almost miraculous acts which were recorded in connection with the conveyance of vast armies overseas and the guns, ammunition and supplies of every sort, without which those armies would have been impotent.

The trawlers and drifters which were taken over by the Admiralty were hired on certain terms, and some interesting details relating to the hire of trawlers were given in the House of Commons in reply to a question as to the rate paid for the trawlers *Southern Prince* and *Ben Arthur*, employed in the Tyne examination service. It was stated that the present rate of payment for the use of these vessels was £475 each per month. The original cost of the *Southern Prince* was £7,200 and of the Ben Arthur £7,000. The total sum paid up to March 31, 1916, for each vessel was approximately £8,200. This included the cost of coal, insurance, stores and repairs, the wages of double crew, and liability for replacement if either vessel was withdrawn for any reason. It was not considered that it would be in the public interest for the department to buy the boats, with all the attendant liabilities.

These details showed that the authorities did not requisition fishing vessels without making what was at least adequate payment; indeed, it happened that fine vessels which had been taken over for Admiralty purposes, and were doing good work, were in course of time paid for at a considerably higher rate than that at which they had been originally secured. This increase proved satisfactory to a number of owners who felt that with their craft employed in the ordinary way of fishing they could have made large sums of money; as it was, they had the further comfort of being assured that their ships were doing invaluable service in the interests of the country, and that in the numerous important ways in which they were employed they were of greater value than if they had been fishing with a fleet or engaged in single-boating.

There were here and there dubious hearts amongst the fishermen; but these were very rare, and the instances related almost exclusively to men who were in the service from necessity and not from the choice which prompted most of the men to go to sea and brave its dangers.

It was the old Dogger spirit that filled the fishermen who were doing naval work and made them fearlessly confront every peril. And some did this who might well have claimed rest ashore; but they were not to be denied an outlet for their abundant energy and loyalty. Numbered amongst these determined souls was a man whose case was uncommonly amusing, but at the same time compelled great admiration. He told the tale himself.

"I'm a curiosity," said the fisherman, who was full of cheerfulness and humour.

"You don't look it," he was told.

"I'm a curiosity," he persisted, "an' I'll tell you why an' show you, then you'll see. I'm in the Navy. I volunteered at the beginnin' of the war. I've had two ships sunk under me, an' last week I was on a vessel that was brought in in a sinkin' condition. It's only just now, after sixteen months, that they've found me out." He gave a joyful laugh. "They did it this way. I had got on finely till one day we were exercisin' and were ordered to double along the deck.

"I said to the officer, 'I can't, sir.'

"His answer was, 'Fall in and double!'

"I said again that I couldn't; then I was reported for insubordination and was taken before the captain.

"The captain said he was sorry to hear that I had refused to obey orders.

"'No, sir,' I said, 'I never refused. I said I couldn't double, an' I can't.'

"'Why can't you?' asked the captain.

"Then I raised my leg and gave a kick, and my foot came off! 'That's why I can't do it, sir,' I told him; and he saw it at once. I had had to have that foot taken off when I was eighteen; but I'd managed very well without it till it came to doublin'.

"Next mornin' I had to show my stump to the ship's surgeon. When I'd done that he said, 'Walk along the deck.' I did so, and he was fair puzzled. 'Which is the stump?' he said. 'Is it the left?'

"'No, sir, it's the right,' I told him, an' pulled off my boot to prove it. An' really you yourself could hardly tell which is which, could you?" he asked, walking about.

Then the fisherman added, with a joyous laugh as he gave a kick and the booted artificial foot came away, "*That's it!* I've got into the knack of doin' it, just as a jokin' surprise! But there it is—an' I'm still in the Navy, the only man, I fancy, that's servin' the king afloat on one

31

foot."

Just as the war called from every nook and corner of the Empire men for the Army, of whom some had led the most peaceful of peaceful lives, so it brought into the naval and fishing services men and lads to whom the busy world was a mysterious and sealed book. Some of these quiet livers had remarkable experiences. Amongst them was a young sailor who came from a fisher home on a small island on the coast of Scotland, a lad who, until he was called up, had never been in a train.

At the end of two months' service, when he had become more or less used to trains and other products of advanced civilisation, he had the shattering experience of being in the worst zone of a night air raid on Chatham in which more than 100 sailors in barracks were killed. He escaped with his life, but had to go into a naval hospital. There was something strikingly impressive in the mental picture of large numbers of these young men and older men from remote home districts who were plunged into the vortex of the conflict. Not a few there were, like this young seaman, who had never travelled in a train, and others who, like the fisherfolk of the Orkneys and Shetlands, made their first acquaintance with the sight of trees.

CHAPTER 3

# The First Sweepers

It is claimed, and perhaps time will show that the claim is not unjustly made, that the employment of nets in connection with the trapping of the earliest of the German submarines originated with an East coast drifter skipper. Let the claim be considered, and it will be obvious that at the least the submarine catching at the outset was a development of the system of catching herrings with the drift-nets.

A "fleet" of nets from a single drifter, it has been shown, could extend a distance of two miles. There were many such drifters in employment when war broke out; many more whose "fleets" in each case would make a vertical wall in the sea a mile and a half long. At the height of the herring season, when the Yare would be packed with drifters and Yarmouth was the centre from which the vessels worked, a round thousand of the craft would be scouring the North Sea and the "fleets" would stretch across from the English to the Jutland coast.

In such a mass of netting it was almost impossible to avoid entanglement, even by skilled skippers, and it sometimes happened that a drifter would get her propeller so hopelessly fouled that she could not steam and had to be towed to port to get the blades set free. The nets were here, there and everywhere, and the more an entangled craft tried to free herself the more securely was her screw made useless and the moment came when the last revolution had been made by the shaft.

Bearing this occurrence in mind, remembering that the German submarines in the beginning were compelled to operate mostly under water, not daring to undertake the more helpful surface tactics which they carried out later, the skipper and those who were of his way of thought propounded the theory that as the drifter became helpless when her propeller was entangled in the herring-nets, so the submarine, in like case, would be powerless; but with this terrible difference, that while a friendly craft could tow the disabled drifter to port the underwater boat was doomed.

In accordance with this theory initial measures were taken which proved of very great value in dealing with German submarines. The unique experience of drifters and trawlermen was brought to bear, and that experience grew enormously as the war progressed.

The skill and experience of the men who had been used to handling ponderous beam-trawls and heavy otter-boards, who had learnt many priceless lessons in constantly dealing with a mile-long steel wire hawser, who had an uncanny knowledge of gallows, God-ends, bridles, bosoms, bellies and other terms describing fishing-gear; who towed their trawls over rough ground and smooth ground, and who knew by instinct when they were on the Silver Pits, or Brucey's Garden or that fatal edge of the Dogger which is notorious as the Cemetery—this skill and experience was the country's for less than the asking. When it was in full operation in connection with the Navy it was put to the delicate and difficult work of sweeping for mines.

This deadly task was carried out by trawlers working in pairs, towing a sweeping-wire which was kept at the required depth by a contrivance called a "kite." The sweeping-wire would catch and hold the steel mooring-wire of a mine, and the infernal machine having been drawn to the surface would be exploded with rifle-fire or by other means. In the beginning this rifle-fire was largely practised by crews of sweepers, and gave them something of relaxation from the sterner work of actual sweeping and forging into grey sinister waters in which an unseen mine might be struck and destroy the sweeper. Being in company afforded much greater protection to the sweepers than would have been the case if working individually.

What the mine-sweepers did in the very early days of the war was shown by an Admiralty *Memorandum* which was issued on February 19, 1915. This publication was a fine tribute to the skill and courage of naval officers and fishermen who had been employed in the dangerous work, and it was of special interest because it put on permanent record details which had been furnished by the admiral commanding the East Coast mine-sweepers of the recent mine-sweeping operations off Scarborough.

The *Memorandum* stated that at the beginning there was no indication of the position of the mines, although, owing to losses of passing merchant ships, it was known that a minefield had been laid. In order

STEAM TRAWLERS MINE-SWEEPING.

THE "GALLOWS" ARE SEEN JUST IN FRONT OF THE FOREMAST.

to ascertain how the mines lay it was necessary to work at all times of tide, with a consequent large increase in the element of danger. These particular operations covered the period from December 19 to December 31, 1914, and were in charge of Commander Richard H. Walters, R.N., A. M.S. Staff. During that time a large number of mines were swept up and destroyed, and by Christmas Day a channel had been cleared, and traffic was able to pass through by daylight.

On the very first day of these dangerous operations Commander Lionel G. Preston, R.N., H.M.S. *Skipjack*, proceeded at once into the middle of the area where some mines had exploded to give assistance to trawlers which had been damaged. He anchored between the trawlers and the mines, which had been brought to the surface, and he set about the work of sinking them.

Lieutenant Godfrey Craik Parsons, R.N., H.M.S. *Pekin*, showed great skill and devotion to duty in continuing to command his group of trawlers after having been mined in Trawler Number 58 on December 19. On that day his group exploded eight mines and brought six more to the surface, Trawler Number 99 being blown up and Numbers 58 and 465 damaged, "all in the space of about ten minutes." That explanation as to time was a clear indication of the strenuous and thrilling nature of the work which Lieutenant Parsons and those who were acting with him did. Special mention was made of Skipper George W. Thornton, of Number 58, which was the trawler *Passing*, for the great coolness he showed and the valuable help he gave Lieutenant Parsons in controlling the crew when the vessel had been mined.

The perilous character of the work was well shown in the case of Lieutenant M. H. Boothby, R.N.R., H.M.S. *Pekin*. He was serving in the trawler *Orianda*, Number 99, on December 19, when she was blown up by a mine. With the exception of one man, who was killed, the officer got all his crew into safety. A few days only were to pass before Lieutenant Boothby had to undergo this unpleasant experience for the second time. On January 6, 1915, he was again blown up in the trawler *The Banyers*, No. 450. *The Banyers* was a fine new vessel of 281 tons and 89 horse-power, built at Beverley in 1914, and she was an example of the numerous powerful up-to-date craft of this description which the Admiralty were able to take over for the purposes of sweeping and other war-work.

Lieutenant C.V. Crossley, R.N.R., also of H.M.S. *Pekin*, performed on that memorable December 19 one of those brave and resourceful acts which became closely associated with the work of sweeping. While sweeping in the trawler *Star of Britain*, three violent explosions occurred close under her stern. The situation was one of very grave danger, but the officer set to work at once to meet it. He "controlled the crew" and then crawled into a confined space near the screw shaft and discovered the damage. Then he managed to stop the leak for the time being well enough to enable the pumps to keep the water down and the ship to be saved.

Little effort of the imagination is needed to picture the courage that was needed to carry out a task like that in a damaged little craft which was in a mine-infested area and might at any moment come in contact with another mine and be utterly destroyed. The circumstances of the work itself also were particularly unfavourable, the screw-shaft of a trawler being necessarily extremely limited.

On the 19th also Lieutenant W. G. Wood, R.N.R., in the trawler *Restrivo*, did excellent work in going to the help of damaged travellers. Amongst other things he performed the risky duty of crossing the minefield at low water when sent to bring in the *Valiant*, which had been disabled by a mine.

Christmas Day provided an opportunity for Skipper T. Tringall, of the trawler *Solon*, to show unommon initiative and bravery. It was night, and a steamer, the *Gallier*, had just been mined. To add to the danger of the situation it was low water; yet these things did not keep Skipper Tringall from going to the help of the mined vessel. This he did on his own responsibility, and his deed was all the more deserving of admiration because the *Gallier* was showing no lights and so had to be searched for in the minefield. It was almost as dangerous an undertaking as looking for an escape of gas with a naked light; yet that was the sort of enterprise on which repeatedly, regardless of personal danger, sweepers and patrollers ventured on many seas throughout the war.

So far the records have dealt with the officers of naval vessels and the trawlers; there remain the details which were published concerning drifters and their crews. It was shown that in the operations there was employed a flotilla of Lowestoft drifters, under Chief Gunner Franklin, R.N. The commodore of this flotilla was Skipper Ernest V. Snowline, in the drifter *Hilda and Ernest*. It was reported of him that he carried out his duties as commodore in a most satisfactory manner, and that he "kept to his station in heavy weather, standing by the s.s. *Gallier* after she had been damaged by a mine." For the same display of devotion to duty in standing by the *Gallier* Skipper William Allerton, of the drifter *Eager*, was specially noticed, and similar recognition was made of Skipper Thomas B. Belton, of the drifter *Retriever*, who kept to his station, marking the safe channel for shipping "when all other drifters were driven in by the weather."

The list of officers mentioned was completed with Sub-Lieutenant W. L. Scott, of the drifter *Principal*, who went alongside the trawler *Garmo* in a dinghy to rescue a man. This he did at considerable risk to himself and his boat, as the trawler was floating nearly vertical at the time, with only the forecastle above water. A few minutes after Scott had left her she turned completely over and sank.

In addition to the officers named, the following were commended for good service done under dangerous conditions:—William A, Lewis, petty officer; Robert Frost, second hand; Edwin F. Frankland, deck hand; Robert A. Gray, Christopher Briggs, George Newman and William R. Kemp, enginemen; and William Gladding, cook. These eight men belonged to mine-sweeping trawlers.

That Memorandum was of singular interest and value, because it showed the earlier methods of dealing with the menace of the mine, and the co-operation between ships of the Navy and the trawlers and drifters. The efficiency of some of the original organisation was proved by the fact that at the beginning of the fourth year of war there were still flotillas of trawlers and drifters with skippers as commodores. In some cases these skippers were offered, and accepted, commissions; but others declined the honour, preferring, for various reasons, to retain the title of "skipper," which had become so well known and valued.

The perils of those early operations amongst the mines was well shown by the cases of H.M.S. *Speedy* and the steam drifter *Linsdell* and H.M.S. *Pathfinder*. On September 3, 1914, the commanding officer of the *Speedy* stated that the *Linsdell* struck a mine that morning 30 miles off the East coast and sank. A quarter of an hour later the *Speedy* also struck a mine and sank. The *Speedy's* casualties were slight. In the case of the drifter, Skipper Woodgate and four members of the crew were missing, the rest of the crew having been picked up by the *Speedy* before she struck the second mine.

Two days later the light cruiser H.M.S. *Pathfinder* struck a mine about twenty miles off the East coast and foundered very rapidly, with heavy loss of life. Several steam drifters which were in the neighbourhood hurried to the scene of the disaster and helped greatly in saving the survivors.

These were amongst the first of the losses which the British Navy sustained through mines, other losses including the battleships *Irresistible* and *Ocean* in the Dardanelles, on March 18, 1915; the battleships *King Edward VII.* and *Russell*, in the Mediterranean; the *Arethusa*, off the East coast, H.M.S. *Lynx*, North Sea, and *Coquette*, East coast; all these losses being due to mines.

The allegation was made that it was Great Britain which first laid a minefield in the middle of the North Sea. This statement was industriously circulated and emphasised by Germany, and it obtained wide credence, especially in neutral countries. Attention was called to the matter in the House of Commons at the beginning of 191 7, and Dr. Macnamara issued a statement with regard to it. "It is so notoriously false as to be ludicrous," he said. Germany began a policy of wholesale mining in the North Sea and the Atlantic from the day war was declared. Many neutral vessels were sunk, and it was only by the exertions of the British Navy that many more were saved. The mines were laid on important neutral trade routes and far out at sea, and no notice of their existence was given. It was not until the beginning of November, 1914, that the first British minefield was laid. The limits of the danger area were at once announced to the whole world, and every possible precaution was taken to prevent any damage to neutral vessels.

That official statement shattered the German lie and was another proof of the exceptional danger to which all ships at sea were exposed because of the promiscuous sowing of mines by the enemy. Germany ran little or no risk, because she had no ships at sea; but the danger to all other countries was grave and became lessened or eliminated only through the persistent skilled efforts of the army of fishermen who were clearing the seas of enemy mines.

During his visit to the Grand Fleet in June, 1917, the king went on board a mine-sweeping trawler which was moored alongside a big warship. From the larger ship the king descended a wooden ladder which led to the sweeper's deck, and there he inspected the crew. Having done this, he shook hands with the skipper and talked freely with the men, asking them various questions concerning their work.

"I am glad to be on board a trawler, amongst you," His Majesty is reported to have said, "and pleased to see you all looking so well after your very hard work."

Inquiring where the men came from, the king was told that they hailed from Aberdeen and other ports.

"And have you had much success in catching and sinking mines?" he asked, to which question a young member of the crew replied that he thought they had had their fair share.

"And how about submarines—any luck with them?" the king continued.

The lad replied, "No, sir, I'm afraid we haven't had any of them down, yet,"

The king asked how they liked the life, and the reply was, "Well, sir, it's a pretty bit rough, but we manage to get through it."

Another mine-sweeper was visited by the king—a brave little ship on the wheelhouse rails of which was boldly displayed the motto, "*What I mine I hold.*" The king was greatly interested in his inspection of the devices employed in sweeping for mines. It was explained to him that the most recent and perfected appliances had to some extent minimised the very great dangers to which the men who sensed in mine-sweepers were exposed.

## CHAPTER 4

# A Skipper's Tale of German Inhumanity

At the very outset of the war the Germans put into operation their threats of "frightfulness"; and against the English in particular they directed their inhuman methods. Fishermen who were peacefully at work offered a target to German naval forces which could not be resisted, and the sinking of defenceless vessels, with the capture of unprotected and powerless toilers were enough to set the German banners of "victory" waving and the German joybells ringing. There were such signs of exultation in the earliest days of the war, when German armed forces swooped upon defenceless British fishermen who were working on the Dogger Bank, and after destroying their vessels, taking the men prisoners to Germany. Amongst these victims was Skipper R. W. Kemp, who, after much suffering as a prisoner of war, was repatriated, and made the revelations which follow.

"I was bound apprentice to the fishing when I was fourteen and a half years old; and I have been to sea close on forty-two years, all the time in fishing craft. I have been master of a vessel ever since I was twenty-five years old. First it was sailing smacks, then it was steam trawlers. Of course I had a lot of the old fleeting days, when smacks went out to the North Sea for eight weeks at a time, and were always out like that with the fleets except when they made short runs home for fresh water and stores and to refit. I was single-boating in the steamboats for a long time, and I was master of a single-boater, the *Lobelia*, when the war broke out.

"I had started from home to earn my livelihood a fortnight before Christmas in 1913, and I worked away up to August, 1914, when the war broke out. We had come into port, Grimsby, not knowing what was going to happen, and lay there for ten days before the insurance people would permit us to go to sea. When we sailed it was on condition that we fished within a certain limit.

"We sailed on August 20, and the day before a friend and myself went for a bit of pleasure to a little country place a few miles from Grimsby.

"We went to sea, and he was blown up by a mine and I was taken prisoner by the Germans, and after sixteen months of shameful treatment was sent home a broken man.

"The *Lobelia* was in the nor'-west corner of the Dogger, what we call the Nor'-West Rough, and there were other steam trawlers about. It was fine, calm summer weather, and we were in good spirits, for we had 160 boxes of fish in the fish-room, the result of five days' fishing. We were making another haul and then we were going home.

"It was three o'clock in the afternoon, and we were hauling. We had got our otter-boards up to the gallows and should soon have had the cod-end of the net unlashed when we saw, all at once, ten torpedo-boats and three cruisers, and as soon as they hove in sight we knew that they were Germans.

"One torpedo-boat rushed up—she was like an eel, and must have done forty knots. She came quite alongside and made her bow rope fast to our bow; then, while the German sailors covered us with revolvers, the commander shouted to me and ordered me to produce the ship's papers. That was all he wanted—he bullied and scurried us about, and would not let us stop to get any of our belongings.

"There was nothing for it but to obey, and so we jumped on board the torpedo-boat, and immediately Germans were sent on board the *Lobelia* and put bombs in her engine-room, then the torpedo-boat cast off and steamed some distance away, and we saw the *Lobelia* blown to pieces.

"All this had happened so swiftly that I could hardly realise it, then I saw that there were other two fishing crews on board the torpedo-boat, and that these craft were scurrying round destroying all the British fishing vessels that they came across. These fishing vessels were absolutely helpless, and had not the slightest chance of escaping or defending themselves.

"It was only ten minutes after we left the *Lobelia* that she blew to pieces, carrying with her every stick and stone that I possessed—and it was the same with the rest of the crew; and in addition to that our 160 boxes of fish and the fish that was in the net—all that we had worked so hard for—went to the bottom. The Germans were in a hurry and wanted to get the job over, and they made no attempt to do anything but get the ship's papers.

"Having done this to the *Lobelia*, the torpedo-boat commander went to another steam trawler—I forget her name, but she was a Grimsby boat—and did the same thing as he had done to us; so we had another fishing crew on board with us, making about forty fishermen in all. We were kept on deck, under an armed guard; but we were allowed to talk amongst ourselves. I must say that while we were prisoners at sea we were treated fairly well, under the circumstances; but once we stepped ashore and got under the military we copped old boots.

"We were on board the torpedo-boat for about six hours, until nine o'clock in the evening. I could never find out her number or any marks on her, and I believe she had none; but, as I say, she was like an eel. Her commander was a young man of about thirty-five years, and he spoke very good English, as so many of these Germans do. He began at once to try and find out things, but we told him nothing.

"He said, 'You have got no men; but we have got the men and we have got the food.' I remember those words.

"The commander asked us a lot of questions about the British Fleet and said he wanted to know the reason why we went to war with Germany; but we could say nothing.

"The sailors gave us something to eat and drink, and we could talk, and were pretty free on board the torpedo-boat—she was not a destroyer; but soon we were to be more strictly treated, and that was when we were transferred to a cruiser. I suppose we were put on board the cruiser because the torpedo-boat was not big enough to house us.

"The cruiser was a tidy size; she had three funnels, but one of them was false.

"We were put down in the forehold of the ship, and armed guards were posted over us. There were portholes in the sides, but the deadlights had been fastened down, so that the only light we had was from lamps. We could not, of course, see anything; but we were kept pretty well informed as to what was going on, and in a curious way, for the pilot came down to see us from time to time and told us what was happening. We knew, because we had seen them, that the cruiser carried a lot of mines on her after deck, and the pilot told us that she was going off the English coast to lay them.

"We afterwards heard that she had thrown them overboard five miles off Blyth and off Flamborough Head; then the cruiser steamed away for Wilhelmshaven, with other ships. But the Germans were about as much afraid of their own mines as they were of ours, for we heard the cable rattle, and the pilot told us that we had brought up under Heligoland, where I had been ashore many a time in the old days of the sailing fleets, when the island was ours. I would have liked a peep at it again, but the Germans took good care that we should see nothing, and we were not allowed on deck.

"There we were, crowded below in the forehold of that cruiser, for two days and nights, with nothing but artificial light, constantly expecting to strike some horrible mine and be blown to pieces. But we were even more afraid of going athwart one of our own warships, for that would have put us down the locker. We should not have had the slightest chance of escape, so we were glad when we knew that we had reached the Wilhelmshaven that the Germans are so proud of.

"What it is really like I don't know—all I saw of it was some tall houses and a lot of shouting women and children, who jeered at us and threw dirt and stones at us—two hundred helpless fishermen, who were marched four deep through the street; for the gallant German Navy had sunk about a score of fishing vessels—ten Grimsby and ten Boston—that could not defend themselves, and had made prisoners of the unarmed crews. Some of these craft had been blown up, as the *Lobelia* had been; others had been sunk with shot. On board the cruiser one of the officers—I do not know his rank—had tried to get something out of us about the British Navy; but he learned no more than the commander of the torpedo-boat had done.

"We soon learned that the 200 fishermen prisoners had been captured by the ten torpedo-boats and three cruisers. They had done the business of sinking the ships, but we did not see all of it, because the trawlers were working over a big area, and most of them were out of sight of the *Lobelia*.

"With German soldiers on each side of us, and the women and boys and girls shouting at us and running after us and pelting us, we were marched through the streets of Wilhelmshaven to a prison—a real prison, and an awful hole at that, and when we got to the lock-up we were thrust into little cells. Each cell was about 8ft. by 5ft., just big enough to cage one man, yet four of us were put in one of the black holes. In my cell there was nothing but a bit of planking on the floor as a bed, but with no bedding of any sort, and a tiny wooden bench.

This cell was like the rest. There were bare stone walls, with no window, and there was no light of any sort, neither lamp nor candle.

"I had never seen the inside of a cell in all my puff, and when I got in there it fairly knocked me on one side altogether. With four of us in such a place there was not room to move. We could not lie on the plank bed and we could not sit on the tiny bench, so we just had to be cramped together, talking and sleeping.

"For four terrible days and nights we were prisoners in these awful cells, our only change being for one hour a day, when, we were allowed to go out on to a green or garden—and a blessed change it was to get out into open air and the sunshine and stretch our aching legs. The sentries brought us our meals, which we ate in the corridor outside the cells. If we wanted to get out for a wash or anything we had to ask leave of the sentries.

"At the end of those four days we had a cruel disappointment. We were only fishermen, who had been captured by German warships and made prisoners. We had nothing whatever to do with the war or fighting—many of the poor chaps had lost everything they had in the world—and we did not see how we could be kept in Germany. We fancied we should be sent home, and, as a matter of fact, we were told that we were going to be sent back. Our very souls sank when the cruel tidings came that, instead of going home, we were to be sent to Sennelager as prisoners of war; and to Sennelager we were taken.

"Things had been bad enough at Wilhelmshaven, in the dark holes of the lock-up, but they were nothing compared with what we had to go through at Sennelager. As soon as we got there we were thrown into the fields, and for three weeks we slept on the grass or the bare ground, for in some places there was no grass. We had no covering, nothing whatever.

"It was during the daytime that we lay on the ground and slept, because then it was warm and dry, with the sun out, and at night, when there were heavy dews, we walked about and tried to keep warm.

"At the end of the three weeks the rainy season came on, and we got tufts of grass and built little huts, about as big as dog-kennels, and crawled into them for shelter.

"The Germans stripped us of everything we had. They would not allow you even a lead pencil or a bit of paper or money; if you had any money they took it from you. But they were not content with that—they disfigured us by cutting one half of the hair of our heads off and one half of the moustache, cropping close and leaving the other half

A POSTCARD FROM A FISHERMAN PRISONER OF WAR.

SCOTCH FISHER-GIRLS BARRELLING HERRINGS.

on, making you as ugly as they could. They took the hair off from the centre of the neck right down to the centre of the forehead, so that those who had long hair looked frightful. This was done out of spitefulness—the Germans don't do it now. It was a nasty thing to do; but we made the best of it, and laughed at one another.

"They fed us very badly.

"For breakfast they gave us coffee, made out of rice, no sugar or milk in it, with nothing to eat. For dinner we had cabbage-water, the cabbage cut up into little bits. Sometimes a little bit of greasy fat pork was put into the water, but it was only by chance that you got one of these bits, about as big as the bowl of your pipe. At teatime you had 'coffee' again, and then you got the black bread, which had to last you twenty-four hours, and that was a piece only as big as your fist.

"When we were taken out of the fields we were put into big canvas tents, holding about 600 men, and there we were packed like sardines in a box. We were forced to lie on the ground, and all sorts of men were crowded together, foreigners and British—far different from the way prisoners of war are treated in England.

"Our being at Sennelager was a great time for the inhabitants, especially on the Sundays, when they would come—Boy Scouts amongst them—and push up to the barbed wire fences and tease and torment us and do all manner of things.

"As time went on we got so that we had no clothing, and no soap, and no means of washing our underclothing. Some of the men 'washed' their shirts by scrubbing them with sand. I tried one day, when it was bitterly cold weather, to 'scrub' my shirt by rubbing it on a bit of a wooden platform we had in the grounds, and it froze so hard to the woodwork that, I could not get it off.

"For the first five or six months we had a cat-and-dog life. The Germans used to hustle us about, kick us, give us a crack with the butt-end of a gun or a prod with a bayonet, and when they were tired of that they would set a big savage dog on to us, a German brute, to hurry us up. The dog used to help the guard when we were hustled along the roadway to the canteen, about half a mile away, to get our dinners. The dog was a sort of man-hunter, and would go for anything. The brute was on a chain, which was held by a soldier, who let him out a certain length; but at times the soldier would slip the chain, so that the dog could fly at a helpless man.

"I saw one of our fishermen cruelly torn in the legs by this savage monster, which had a craze for rushing at poor chaps from behind.

And you dared not touch the beast or complain or do anything, if you did you suffered for it.

"The poor fellow that the brute bit complained to the head commander, and there was an inquiry on the job. And what happened? The man got lashed to a tree for two hours in the morning and two hours in the afternoon for complaining! And that was in the wintertime. He is now at home, but he still suffers a great deal with it, and was in hospital in Germany a lot because of the bites and the lashing to the tree.

"Can you wonder that as the result of such brutal and inhuman treatment men died through sheer exhaustion? They did. Several of our poor fishermen died, and they are buried in Germany—all through privation.

"In the winter we used to go about with our knees through our trousers, and we had no jackets to wear. I never had a pair of stockings or socks for the whole time I was there. My feet were wrapped up in rags, with old wooden Dutchman's shoes.

"In time the Germans provided us with barracks, but we still had to lie on the ground. We lay on the ground for the whole of the sixteen months I was in Germany. We just had straw—we had nothing to cover ourselves with, no blankets or anything. The only way to keep warm was to keep as close together as sardines. They used to place us like this—one Englishman, one German, one Russian and one Frenchman, to keep you by yourself, so that you should not have your own countryman to talk to.

"Some of the prisoners used to have to go to work trench digging, pulling roots of trees out of the ground, and so on. I did the root-pulling, but I got nothing whatever for it. We used to drip in the warm weather. All our food was drink, drink, drink. There was no stayable food all the time I was there, and if it had not been for the help from good friends in England we should certainly have starved altogether.

"We used to have to form up in the morning, and if you did not keep exactly straight in line you got punished. They would make you run round a pole with half a dozen bricks on your back, or dig the ground with a shovel, with the same burden. And they used to go through a form of inspection with you, forcing you to be stark naked, no matter what the weather was like.

"We were driven about like sheep, and for the first five months of our imprisonment we were not allowed to write or receive letters, and when at last we were given liberty to write home the Germans either destroyed the letters or would not let them go. This meant that your people at home were in an agony of doubt all the time as to what had happened to you, and did not know whether you were alive or dead.

"After a whole year of this sort of suffering at Sennelager I was transferred, with other fishermen, to Ruhleben, which was an exchange depot. This was the first time the Germans had allowed seafaring men to be exchanged, and we were only allowed to go as the result of a visit to Sennelager which the American Ambassador had made. Men over fifty-five and lads under seventeen were in the exchange.

"I learned in time that there were eighty-five of us fishermen prisoners to be allowed to come home in exchange, and that the ages ranged from sixty years to fourteen—yes, there were mere boys as prisoners. One came home when I did. He was just under seventeen; but there were younger lads as prisoners, and they were treated exactly like the men. I am glad to say that we had not a boy on board the *Lobelia*. Fancy treating little chaps like that!

"Some of our chaps were a bit obstinate, and they got the worst punishment. The Germans were all push and drive, and if you didn't show yourself willing to do just as you were told, and turned sulky, well, shoot them—that was the order. I saw two or three Belgians and Frenchmen shot just for this offence, turning sulky and refusing to obey orders. There was no sort of court-martial or trial about it; they were shot where they stood.

"A very common punishment was to lash the men to trees and make them work with the load of bricks on their backs, as I have described—the Germans were rare boys for that sort of business. At Sennelager there were only 200 British fishermen prisoners of war, but there were 2,300 Russian, Belgian, and French prisoners, all civilians, some of them *burgomasters* and so on. And they were rough uns, too, some of them; but that was no excuse for the terrible punishments which the Germans carried out.

"All the time we were in the camps we were never allowed any information or newspapers, except about German victories. They had a pole, and when they had a bit of a victory they flew all the flags they could put on it—and they put a birch-broom on the top of the pole, after the style of Old Tromp when he boasted that he had swept the English from the seas. The Germans hadn't done that, but they used to make a rare to do if they got a little advantage at all.

"For twelve months out of the sixteen during which I was a prisoner we never saw a knife, fork, or spoon. We had to walk about half a mile for our dinner, such as it was, and stand in a crowd, like a mob, to get it. When we had had the stuff served out we used to scoop it up the best way we could, with an oyster shell or a bit of tin, or anything else that we were lucky enough to pick up from the ground.

"I got back to my home on Christmas Day, after an absence of more than two years. Had I had enough of it? Yes, so far as imprisonment goes; but if I had not been too old I should have done as a lot of my old friends have done—gone mine-sweeping. Instead of being able to do that I had to take a shore job inland, so I am still away from my home, and likely to be. Winter is coming on again; it takes me an hour to walk to my work and an hour to walk back, and as the result of my sufferings as a prisoner of war in Germany I have bad rheumatism. However, I am still here—which is more than I can say for my poor friend who went out with me for a bit of pleasure and was soon blown up by a mine. And there are still six of the *Lobelia's* crew prisoners in Germany, only four of us having been exchanged and allowed to come home.

"When I went away to fish I had everything.

"I came home a wreck.

"And that is what the war has done for me."

CHAPTER 5

# War on Fishing Craft

Throughout the war the Germans did their utmost, by every means at their disposal, to destroy their enemies' fishing vessels, and particularly British craft. No consideration of humanity or law restrained them. They deliberately fired upon and sank steam and sailing fishing vessels that were engaged solely in fishing; in very many cases they forced crews to abandon their vessels and take their chance of safety in the small boats; and they committed acts which were equivalent to wilful murder. In these operations they were as cowardly as they were merciless, for no courage was needed to attack a fishing vessel which had not so much as an old blunderbuss on board.

A cluster of fishing craft, peacefully at work, offered a target which was wholly to the liking of the commander of an enemy submarine or other war vessel. His brave German heart throbbed exultantly, for here was an adventure which involved no peril that he could not easily avert, and the assurance of much applause, and at least an Iron Cross. He rejoiced if he sank fishing vessels wholesale—one German commander boasted, and there was no good reason to doubt his claim, that he had himself sunk English fishing vessels of the value of £150,000. Very heavy losses undoubtedly were inflicted by individual German commanders who had at their disposal the most terrible and destructive of naval weapons and did not scruple to employ it ruthlessly.

The object of this policy of piracy was two-fold—to instil fear in the British people through "frightfulness," and by removing fishing vessels to lessen the supply of food. The first object was never attained, even remotely; and the second was nullified by the persistence of British fishermen in going to sea and their obstinate refusal to keep away from it at the bidding of any enemy whatsoever.

Fish was dear—the "profiteers" were said to be largely responsible for that—but at most times there was plenty of it, and a scarcity was generally due to bad weather and not to any fear of Germans. There was an inevitable falling off in the supplies compared with pre-war days, because the fishing areas were so greatly restricted and most of the fishing vessels and their crews were on Admiralty service; but large quantities of fish, of a very high value, continued to be brought into port. In August, 1917, 10,414 tons of fish were delivered at Billingsgate, and large supplies were steadily brought into ports around the coast. These landings were a proof of the courage of the men who made them and of the failure of the German methods of ruthlessness.

When war broke out four steam fleets were fishing in the North Sea—the Great Northern, the Red Cross, the Gamecock, and Messrs. Hellyers'. The Red Cross and Great Northern fleets had existed for nearly forty years, but only during part of that time exclusively as steam trawlers, and the other fleets had been at work for long un-broken periods. These fleets were quietly withdrawn, the immediate result being that the principal fishing ports were crowded with craft for which there was no work, and heavy financial loss was suffered by owners and fishermen. That state of things, however, was soon to be remedied, and the ships and men who might have suffered severely through German attacks were absorbed for naval work. Owing to this precaution the Germans were not able to run amok in the fleets; but there were still many vessels single-boating at considerable distances from land, and often enough working close together.

By wantonly attacking these fishing vessels the Germans in a very short period inflicted heavy losses, and in less than three months Grimsby alone had lost a large number of vessels and men through direct attack, in addition to losses caused by mines. A list of known losses contained 27 steam trawlers, with 83 men dead and 128 pris-oners—a total of 211. Between 80 and 90 of the prisoners were mar-ried men. This list was composed of thirteen trawlers destroyed, their crews of nine—in two cases ten—being made prisoners; one trawler captured and destroyed, the crew being brought home; one captured, with her crew of nine, and seven trawlers missing, probably lost with all hands—of these seven vessels five had a crew of nine, one of ten, and one of twelve; five trawlers were reported sunk through mines, one vessel losing seven out of nine men, and another six out of nine. In another case one man only was lost, eight being saved.

These figures showed the uncertain action of mines. A mine ex-ploding might and often did cause the total disappearance of a vessel and her crew, it might badly damage a ship and kill and maim some of her people, or it might do serious but not irreparable mischief, and yet spare the crew altogether. Much depended on the part of the vessel which was struck—and mines exploded everywhere.

That early list, heavy and serious, was soon enlarged, and it grew steadily as the war proceeded. Similar lists relating to other ports increased in proportion, but never was even a murmur heard of ceasing or slackening the efforts which were being made at sea to hold the enemy in check and crush him; never a thought disturbed the fishermen, combatant or non-combatant, except that of "sticking it" and final victory.

The first Christmas of the war brought heavy shadows to many travellers' homes. The German mine-laying after the raid on Scarborough was undoubtedly the cause of many losses amongst trawlers and sweepers. The news of the loss of the *Ocana*, through a mine, reached Grimsby on Christmas Eve, just as preparations had been made for the men's home-coming for Christmas; and the mine-sweeper *Night Hawk* was lost on Christmas Day. By that time 123 fishermen were prisoners of war in Germany and were learning too well what it meant to fall into the power of people whose creed was that of blood and iron and its resultant "frightfulness."

What some of these losses meant was shown by the case of James Coleman, deck-hand of the *Balmoral*. She left Grimsby on January 23, 1915, and was never heard of. Coleman left eight children. In the previous November a son of his was killed while fighting for his country in France, and not long before that another son was washed overboard from a trawler and drowned. So, in the course of a few months death had claimed the father and two sons—and the eldest son also was serving as a soldier.

Such losses were not uncommon. They were crushingly severe; but the heavy burden was greatly lightened by the knowledge that the men had fallen in a good fight, and the practical sympathy which was shown by the public, which was beginning at last to understand how vast a debt it owed to fishermen of every sort.

An illustration of German "frightfulness" was afforded by the loss of the Grimsby trawler *Vanilla*, which was destroyed by a German submarine, her entire crew of nine being lost with her. The tragic tale of her sacrifice was told by the skipper of another Grimsby trawler, the *Fermo*, which was in the company of the *Vanilla*. The skipper said that the two vessels were fishing at a spot near the area in which the trawler *Zarina* had been blown up some time previously.

On a Sunday afternoon in April, 1915, the skipper and members of his crew saw a submarine rise to the surface, but keeping her deck awash. The *Vanilla* had got part of her gear on board, when, without any warning, the submarine discharged a torpedo at her.

A terrible explosion followed, and the *Vanilla* was blown to pieces. When the water, which had been raised in a huge mass and spray, had fallen, the horrified watchers saw that the *Vanilla* had completely disappeared.

When this happened the skipper of the *Fermo* and his crew were hauling their gear; they worked with frantic energy to complete their task, and when it was done and the net was on deck the boat was launched and he put on steam to go to the assistance of anyone who might have escaped death from the explosion.

The *Fermo* steamed amongst the wreckage, but there was not a sign of any member of the torpedoed trawler's people, nor did the skipper expect to find any survivor of such a catastrophe. All the crew must have been killed instantly. Then, almost alongside his own vessel, the skipper saw another submarine—at one time, he declared, so close to him that he could almost have touched it, and if he had not been so intent on trying to save possible survivors he could easily have rammed the craft.

The *Fermo* herself was now put in extreme peril, for when only four or five hundred yards separated her from the submarine a torpedo was fired at the trawler. Most fortunately it failed to strike.

The submarine then turned and began to chase the *Fermo*, which was now being kept at full speed. That was the beginning of a struggle which lasted four hours—a contest between a German murderer and a North Sea skipper. By coolness, skill and grim courage the skipper managed to elude his cowardly pursuer, and after an exhausting chase the submarine was lost to sight. That was at seven o'clock in the evening—a peaceful Sabbath when the church bells were ringing ashore—and finally the *Fermo* reached Grimsby safely.

As to the identity of the submarines the skipper said that there was no chance to see either letters or numbers, as both vessels kept partly submerged until the chase of the *Fermio* began, and none of the crews came on deck. He emphasised the fact that the *Vanilla* never had an opportunity to do anything, and quite possibly her crew were not aware of the presence of the first submarine.

From the *Fermo's* deck the *Vanilla's* people could be seen hauling their gear when the torpedo struck her. In an instant she had vanished, leaving only pieces of wreckage far and wide upon the water.

This case was one of deliberate murder, so monstrous in its conception, that even the German who was responsible for its execution must have felt at least some tinge of pity for the helpless toilers of the deep whom he was ruthlessly destroying. For cruel deliberation and pitilessness nothing could exceed this appalling crime, one of many like it. There was the peaceful Sunday, the inoffensive, unarmed fishing vessel at work, the unsuspecting crew; yet up to such the submarine made its deadly way, fired its annihilating weapon, and shattered a ship and blew to pieces nine gallant, hard-working men, making already heavily-burdened women widows and dependent children orphans. It was in this direction especially that these murders told distressingly on the fishing community—at about that period another Grimsby trawler, the *Horatio*, was torpedoed and lost with all hands. She carried a crew of fourteen, of whom no fewer than eleven were married.

For these infamies, which forever blackened and degraded the name of German seamen, there was not and could not be any excuse except that of the necessity which knew no law. Germany made it clear that she had deliberately thrown to the winds all the restraint which humanity and honour impose on belligerents; she sank to depths which had never been plumbed even by Goths and Huns—the veneer of civilisation slipped easily off this parvenu amongst the nations. The Germans announced that as part of their naval plan of campaign they would proceed against fishing vessels with even greater energy than before, and they kept their dishonourable word.

One glorious spot shone in that Sunday tragedy of the *Vanilla*— and it was the courage shown by the skipper of the *Fermo* and his crew in steaming up to the place where the trawler had been torpedoed, bent on rescue. Fearlessness and skill, those famous attributes of the deep sea men, were shown at their best, and if rescue had been possible, rescue would have been accomplished, in spite of all the infamies of Germany. This fortitude and bravery was not isolated—numberless cases occurred of life-saving by fishermen when losses had been inflicted by vessels of the enemy. In some cases these displays were suitably honoured; in many instances they had to be added to that long list of good deeds done on the North Sea being their own reward.

An announcement by the Secretary to the Admiralty showed that up to March 17, 1915, 28 fishing vessels had been sunk or captured and 19 lost by mines since the war began—making a total of 47. The heaviest losses were in the weeks which ended on August 26 and November 4. In the first-named period no fewer than 24 fishing vessels were lost through the action of enemy vessels of all classes, and in the November week five fishing vessels were lost through mines; the total gross lost tonnage for the two weeks being 4,141 and 583 respectively. The August week was that in which the Germans swooped on the inoffensive fishermen, sank some of the helpless vessels and captured other craft. There was reason to believe that these captured trawlers were afterwards treacherously used by the Germans in mine-laying and covering submarine attacks.

When the unrestricted operations of the German submarines began early in 1917 there were many losses of fishing vessels. The losses were very heavy in March and April, being 40 and 38 respectively; they became much lighter in the summer months, possibly because the Germans found bigger ships to operate against. In May the fishing craft lost numbered 23; other totals were: June, 23; July, 15; August, 5; September, 7; October, 5. The total losses from February 25 to December 22, inclusive, were 167. The total for fifty-eight weeks was 198.

No feelings of humanity were allowed to interfere with the murderous work which the German submarine commanders had been ordered to carry out. These craven craft often worked at long distances from the German bases, and their crews had not the slightest disposition to accept any risk in adhering to the unwritten immemorial laws which had ruled at sea amongst combatants.

No parallel for the German ferocity was to be found except in the black annals of piracy. The German submarines lay in wait off peaceful ports for inoffensive fishing craft, and these, as a rule, they sank at sight, leaving the crews to take the meagre chance of salvation which a small boat or a piece of wreckage afforded.

In the winter of 1916 no fewer than sixteen fishing vessels were lost through enemy action off a quiet West Coast fishing port. The vessels were merely fishing in the ordinary way; but that did not secure for them any immunity or safety, and with several smacks that disappeared the crews perished. It spoke well for the kindness and devotion of the survivors that three of them began to make a collection for the women and children who had been widowed and orphaned, and by this method they collected nearly £71; other efforts increasing the amount to over £110. This money was carefully administered over a period of a year, and it was employed in helping three widows and sixteen children whose menfolk had been lost with a smack that sailed from the same port and was torpedoed.

These tragedies emphasised the dangers that were consistently faced by men who were fishing in what might reasonably have been looked upon as "safe" zones.

Repeated attempts were made by German airships at sea to destroy British fishing vessels. These airships often hovered over the North Sea, in carrying out their reconnoitring work. As a rule they had a wholesome dread of British warships, but they seemed to have a singular partiality for trying to destroy small unarmed vessels, and many stories were told of escapes from these aerial attacks which were due to the coolness and resource of the fishermen.

On one occasion incoming trawlers at Grimsby reported that they had sighted four Zeppelins hovering over the North Sea, apparently waiting for dusk before attempting a raid on England.

One of the airships was seen to bear the mark L11, and this vessel manoeuvred with the object of getting over the trawler *Adelaide*, presumably to bomb her. Seeing this purpose the skipper cut away his gear, and freed of this great dragging obstacle he was able to get full speed on his steamboat and by continuous zigzagging to escape.

Baffled in this effort, the airship attacked another of the trawlers, the *Lyrine*, and very nearly succeeded in destroying her, for a bomb which was dropped missed the little fishing craft by only about thirty yards.

IN A FLEET OF STEAM TRAWLERS.

## CHAPTER 6

# Trawlers to the Rescue

Grievous though some of the losses of warships and their crews were, yet these calamities were lessened by the help which fishermen were able to give. In very many cases the fishermen were serving in mine-sweepers; but many others were doing their ordinary work of catching fish or were on their way to or from port. Wherever they were or whatever they were doing became immaterial if need arose to bear a hand in saving life from a ship in distress through enemy attack or striking a mine or any other cause.

Very prominent amongst these cases of rescue was that of the battleship *Formidable*, which was sunk in the Channel on New Year's Day, 1915, with great loss of life; a loss which would have been much heavier but for the courage and fine seamanship shown by Skipper William Pillar and his crew in the trawler *Provident.* A singular circumstance in connection with this affair was the persistence with which the vessel was described as the *Providence*; newspapers and historical works perpetuating the mistake. The *Provident* was a typical Brixham beam-trawler, owned as well as skippered by Pillar. Her mate was William Carter; John Clarke was the second hand; and the boy was Daniel Taylor, commonly known as Dan,

January 1 was ushered in by a bitter gale in the Channel. The *Formidable* was torpedoed by a German submarine and foundered, 600 of her complement of 800 perishing. Seventy-one of the rescued men were picked up from a swamped cutter by the *Provident* and carried into Brixham. Seventeen of the survivors were taken to the Fishermen's Institute, to which Brixham women took beds and bedding for their use, recalling the incident of the great storm in 1866, when the women of Brixham made bonfires with their bedding, to light in the men who were in peril on the sea. From these survivors came some of the earliest information of the disaster to the *Formidable* and the heroism of the trawler's crew. Subsequent details completed the story.

The first intimation of the loss of the *Formidable* was in the following report from the Admiralty:—

The battleship *Formidable* was sunk this morning in the Channel, whether by mine or submarine is not yet certain. Seventy-one survivors have been picked up by a British light cruiser, and it is possible that others may have been rescued by other vessels.

This hope was fulfilled by the subsequent arrival in port of the *Provident*. It was then known that the smack, after three hours' strenuous work in the bitter weather and dangerous seas, had effected her rescues.

The *Provident* was at sea, about fifteen miles from Berry Head. Owing to the heavy weather she was running to Brixham for shelter; but when off the Start she was forced to heave to. Already she had been struck by heavy seas. When on the starboard tack Clarke noticed an open boat under the smack's lee. He shouted to the skipper and the mate to jump up, saying, "Here's a sight under our lee!" When they looked they saw an open boat driving through the heavy seas. An oar was hoisted as a mast, and from this a sailor's scarf was flying. For minutes together the boat was hidden from view; but the men of the *Provident* had got her and were determined that she should not be allowed to go. The skipper swung the smack clear, then he and his small band set to work to take in another reef in the mainsail and set the storm-jib. Until this had been done it would have been disastrous to attempt a rescue.

The boat, which was one of the battleship's cutters, drifted towards the smack, from which she was seen by Clarke, who had climbed the rigging.

The skipper decided to gybe, a perilous manoeuvre in such weather, as the mast was liable to give way; but he succeeded. Four times the smacksmen tried to get a rope to the cutter; each attempt being more difficult than the last; but finally they obtained a good berth on the port tack. A small warp was thrown and caught by the sailors in the cutter, and this having been made fast round the capstan the boat was hauled to the stern of the *Provident*. The warp was passed round to the lee side and the boat was brought up to the lee quarter.

So far so good. The first part of the fight had been won. The cutter had been secured and there was every prospect of saving the men who were crowded into it, swept by the icy seas, and suffering severely, for they had been in the boat for twelve hours, and were very insufficiently clothed.

The sailors watched for their chance of jumping and climbing on board the heaving smack from their own little vessel, which was riotously thrown about by the seas—it was calculated that the seas at times rose to a height of thirty feet, so that the cutter was often in a deep hollow or high above the *Provident*. But the skill and coolness of the skipper and his crew, and the strong efforts of the shipwrecked men who saw safety so near, proved successful, and after a stirring and tumultuous fight of half-an-hour the survivors in the boat were safe on board the smack. Considering the perils of the situation, the work of transfer was done with remarkable freedom from casualties; the most serious injury being caused by a man's fingers getting jammed between the cutter and the smack.

The little *Provident* was crowded when she had taken on board the seventy-one men who had been packed in the boat, but in the prompt way of the fisherman, who was so accustomed to deal ably with emergencies, instant steps were taken to provide relief for the sufferers. Amongst these was a lad of eighteen who needed immediate care so that his life should be saved.

Torpedo-Gunner Hurrigan, who was in charge of the cutter, was the last to leave her, getting on board the smack by means of the mizen rigging. When he had left the boat the rope was cut; but the little craft had done its work well. She was full of water, having a hole in her which had been stuffed with a pair of pants, one of the sailors having taken off these garments for the purpose. As soon as the men had been got on board the *Provident* headed for Brixham. This was at one o'clock in the afternoon. A fifty-ton sailing smack could not afford much accommodation for nearly eighty men, all told; but she provided welcome shelter to men who were almost perishing and starving, and whatever it was possible for the fishermen to do for the sufferers they did.

There was the little cabin itself, which was crowded, so was the fish-room, the hold also, where the boiler was installed; and the warmth below was welcome indeed to men who for so many hours had been battling with a winter gale in an open boat, constantly expecting death. They had nothing to eat or drink, and their clothing was of the scantiest, for the torpedoing of a battleship left no time to dress. In some cases the rescued men had no trousers, and these were allowed to take the places nearest to the boiler fire. Other men were bare-footed, and all suffered greatly from exposure. Welcome indeed, therefore, was the shelter and warmth of the smack's interior, and as welcome the hot coffee and biscuits which were provided on board. To these comforts were added the knowledge that Brixham fishermen had a Brixham smack in charge and that they were running for a safe old Channel port. That knowledge was inexpressibly encouraging to the men who had endured so much and had been so skilfully and courageously saved. The rescue, said one of the survivors, was a wonderful piece of work.

Nothing held the *Provident* back. She kept steadily on her course, and between seven and eight o'clock she was safe in Brixham Harbour, and was taken alongside the quay by a tug. Immediately every possible help was given to the battleship's survivors, and as a result of the doctoring, nursing, clothing, feeding and sleeping that they enjoyed, they quickly pulled round and were made fit to take their places again in the fighting forces.

Other boats were able to get away from the foundering battleship, amongst them the pinnace, containing 57 men. This boat was full of water at the start. From half-past two in the morning until eleven at night these men were exposed to the wind and seas, and though there were no losses through physical injury half-a-dozen men died in the boat, and when the survivors got ashore three more died. This fate would probably have overtaken at least some of the men in the cutter if it had not been for the gallant rescue by the crew of the *Provident*.

The conduct of the skipper and his little band called public attention to the case, and afterwards the Admiralty decided to recognise the gallantry by awarding £250 to the skipper, £100 each to Carter and Clarke, and £50 to the boy Dan. Other monetary rewards and the Shipwrecked Mariners' Society's medals were also awarded to the men, who had again proved the value of fishermen in time of war.

At Buckingham Palace, later, the skipper and his crew were received by the king, who said: "I congratulate you heartily upon your gallant and heroic conduct. It is a great feat to have saved seventy-one lives. I realise how difficult your task must have been, because I know myself how arduous it is to gybe a vessel in a heavy gale."

From the very beginning of the war it was almost a matter of course that life-saving operations at sea included splendid work by trawlers and other fishing vessels. These acts were not in most cases of the nature which so specially called attention to the *Provident* and her crew; but they invariably involved the display of uncommon courage and skill.

Foremost amongst these doings was the behaviour of trawlers in connection with the deplorable loss of the three cruisers, *Aboukir*, *Cressy* and *Hogue* on the morning of September 22, 1914. These were sister ships of 12,000 tons and 18 knots, and the circumstances of their loss created a widespread and painful impression. It was considered advisable by the Admiralty to issue a statement with reference to the sinking of the cruisers, and accordingly the Secretary of the Admiralty published one. The Admiralty said that the facts of the affair could not be better conveyed to the public than by the reports of the senior officers who had survived and landed in England.

> The sinking of the *Aboukir* was, of course, an ordinary hazard of patrolling duty. The *Hogue* and *Cressy*, however, were sunk because they proceeded to the assistance of their consort, and remained with engines stopped endeavouring to save life, thus presenting an easy and certain target to further submarine attacks. The natural promptings of humanity have in this case led to heavy losses which would have been avoided by a strict adherence to military considerations.

The Secretary of the Admiralty added that it had become necessary to point out, for the future guidance of His Majesty's ships, that the conditions which prevailed when one vessel of a squadron was injured in a minefield, or was exposed to submarine attack, were analogous to those that occurred in an action, and that the rule of leaving disabled ships to their own resources was applicable, so far, at any rate, as large vessels were concerned. Small craft of all kinds, however, should be directed by wireless to close the damaged ship with all speed.

The Germans claimed that the whole of the torpedoing was done by one submarine; but not a few of the survivors declared that several submarines were at work. In any case, three fine ships were totally lost, with nearly 60 officers and 1,400 men. Many of these brave sailors perished instantly, others died in the water or from their injuries; but 60 officers and 779 men were saved. Of that considerable total no fewer than 156 officers and men were picked up by Skipper Phillips and his crew in the trawler *L. T. Coriander*; these fishermen doing splendid service and winning the warm praise of Commander Bertram W. L. Nicholson, of the *Cressy*. A Lowestoft trawler and two

Dutch ships, the *Flora* and *Titan*, were extraordinarily kind, reported Commander Reginald A. Norton, of the *Hogue*; but he had to add that a Dutch sailing trawler sailed close by without rendering any assistance, though they signalled to her from the *Hogue* to close, after they were struck. Not a few of the survivors were satisfied that this supposed Dutch fishing vessel was not Dutch at all, but a German vessel sailing under false colours, and for the credit of Holland and her fishermen it was hoped that this suspicion was correct.

The shock of the loss of the three cruisers had scarcely passed when the Admiralty announced the loss of H.M.S. *Hawke*. This was in October, 1914. H.M.S. *Theseus* and the *Hawke* were attacked by submarines "in the northern waters of the North Sea." The *Theseus* was missed, but the *Hawke* was sunk, with the loss of nearly 500 lives. The announcement added that three officers and 49 men of the *Hawke's* crew had been landed at Aberdeen by a trawler. This vessel was the *Ben Rinnes*, Skipper John Cormack, who, on landing the survivors at Aberdeen Fish Market, stated that he had taken them off a Norwegian steamer on the previous night.

Though this was not a direct rescue by a steam trawler, it was an instance of the ubiquity of these vessels and the great help they gave in relieving other ships of unexpected passengers. The trawler was able to take the survivors to port and the neutral steamer was at liberty to continue her voyage unencumbered and unembarrassed. These survivors, the skipper stated, had escaped in an overcrowded boat, but nothing could be done to save the men who were floating in the water with cork jackets or who were on rafts. The periscope of the attacking submarine disappeared immediately after the explosion.

There was practically no form of warfare in which fishermen did not take a part of some sort, and the raids by German airships were not an exception. On the night of January 31, 1916, some of the Eastern and Midland counties of England were raided by enemy airships, and a number of men, women and children were killed and property was seriously damaged. The airships escaped from England, but one of them was found floating on the North Sea, a helpless wreck. All that was known at the time was that the discovery was made by the skipper and crew of the *King Stephen*, a Grimsby steam trawler, that the circumstances prevented the skipper from doing more than reporting the matter to the Naval authorities, and that the wrecked raiders perished. It soon became known, however, that the occurrence was one of the most dramatic happenings of the aerial warfare and that the German raiders in this case had met a terrible but well-deserved fate.

The published details showed that the wrecked airship was seen by, the *King Stephen*, and that on going to the spot the skipper and his people counted no fewer than twenty-two Germans. These men implored the skipper to rescue them, but as the *King Stephen* was entirely unarmed and carried only nine hands, and as there had been such overwhelming proof of German treachery and inhumanity in relation to fishermen, especially on the North Sea, the skipper rightly enough declined to put himself and his crew in the power of an enemy whose word was worthless and who undoubtedly, if he had had the chance to do so, would have seized the vessel and done his best to escape with her as a prize and the crew as prisoners.

Unwillingly enough the skipper had to refuse to take the Germans on board his little vessel; but he steamed away, and without delay informed naval vessels which he came across of the discovery that he had made. Not a moment was lost by these ships in going to the scene of the disaster, but no vessel was in time to save the Germans, who, with their shattered airship, had perished in the waters which they had so recently crossed on their murderous visit to unprotected English towns and villages.

When the circumstances of this case became known in Germany there was the inevitable allegation of cowardice and inhumanity against British fishermen. The charge was baseless and unsupported by the facts, the truth being that on repeated occasions British fishermen had shown the utmost courage and had run very grave risks in rescuing German sailors who had been shipwrecked, and in not a few instances their gallantry had been so marked that special presents, such as gold watches and binoculars, had been presented by the *Kaiser* to British skippers and other fishermen.

Not long after this particular occurrence another German airship which had been wrecked off the mouth of the Thames was discovered by an auxiliary patrol trawler, so that within the period of a few weeks trawlers in a very remarkable manner had become associated with the inglorious fate of German air raiders.

## CHAPTER 7

# Heroic Deeds

The men of the trawlers and drifters who in time of peace had drawn a hard-won living from the deep sea were never prone to talk of what they had seen and done; and war did not change their silence. In happier times they came ashore in little brotherly bands or stayed on board in similar fraternal clusters, and made the best of their confinement.

The fisherman as such was akin to the creatures he pursued and captured, for he, like many of them, foregathered and worked in shoals. He did not amalgamate, and was not to be assimilated. He was largely a worker alone, a species apart, and no ordinary seaman's or mariner's resort attracted him; he was drawn only by some place which existed solely for the benefit of fishermen.

This limpet-like attachment of the fisher for his home gave rise to the famous instance of the stranger who inquired in a Buchan coast village for one Alexander White.

"Could you tell me far Sanny Fite lives?" he asked a girl he met.

"Filk Sanny Fite?" inquired the maiden, helpfully.

"Muckle Sanny Fite," replied the stranger, illuminatingly.

"Filk Muckle Sanny Fite?" persisted the native, impatiently.

"Muckle lang Sanny Fite," answered the inquirer, desperately.

"Filk muckle lang Sanny Fite?" demanded the girl, remorselessly.

"Muckle lang gleyed Sanny Fite!" shouted the man, as a forlorn hope.

"Oh!" exclaimed the informant contemptuously. "It's 'Goup-the-Lift' ye're seekin'—an' fat for dinna ye speer for the man by his richt name at ance?"

In war-time the fisherman maintained the customs which he had loved in times of peace, and at naval bases to which he was attached he could be seen, especially on Sundays, wandering in understanding companionship about the quays, or docks, or streets, but never far from his vessel, which held him like a magnet. She was there, right enough, often looking as if she would remain undisturbed until many wars had ended; but the uniformed bands soon reappeared, took reassurance of the actual continued presence of the little ship, and strolled away again, or gazed in meditation at the familiar floating object.

"I don't know the place, and I can't tell you anything about it," said a skipper at a base, answering a question as to guidance. "Besides, I'm only just in from the Mediterranean. I could tell you more about Aberdeen." And with a kind but uninformative smile on his bronzed, hard-set face he strolled away, not without a backward glance at his beloved drifter, which he had just left, and which was in the company of other little drifters, one or two with wireless fitted, and each with the tiny gun mounted, the like of which had proved so effective against Germans, Austrians and other enemies.

What could not that skipper have told of himself, his crew and his wonderful steam-propelled wooden tub which bore the registry letters of a Scotch port 600 miles away, and had braved the Biscay at the time of autumn gales? Yet if he told a tale at all it would surely be in curt replies to questions, and then only when he was forced to answer. However great his achievements might be, they would have no record from his own mouth; and as it was with him so it was with most of his fellows, the result being that almost the only published stories were those which were officially prepared and based on information possessed by the authorities.

Examples of sweepers and patrollers' heroic deeds have been given in previous chapters, and the tale in this respect is continued.

There is a fine old British regimental motto which declares that no dangers daunt, and it could be well applied to many of the *personnel* of the mine-sweeping service, other than the actual fishermen. Such a case was afforded in a number of incidents taken from Admiralty records and officially made known for the encouragement of the public. It related to the extraordinary act of an unnamed lieutenant of the Royal Naval Volunteer Reserve. He was in command of a motor launch attending on a flotilla of mine-sweeping trawlers when a drifting mine was sighted. Half a gale was blowing and a heavy sea was running, and not only had attempts to sink the mine by gunfire proved abortive, but it was getting dark, and there was a strong probability that the mine would be lost sight of and drift away and remain a peril to navigation.

The lieutenant, determined to do his best to remove the danger, lowered a boat and pulled over to the mine, which was only occasionally to be seen as it was swept by the waves. The officer got as close to the mine as he dared to pull, then he jumped into the sea with a line, which he passed through the ring-bolt in the top of the mine. This line was made fast to the motor launch, which towed the mine into smooth water, where it was sunk by rifle fire.

The uncommon coolness and courage of this act is obvious, for in the turmoil of wind and sea the officer might well have inadvertently seized one of the horns of the mine and ended the enterprise in a manner far different from the purpose which he had in mind.

This thrilling incident was made known in the autumn of 1917, when a selection of such cases had been published, and had given a glimpse, but a glimpse only, of the work of those who swept and kept the seas. Though when the story was published there was no mention of the officer's name, yet a number of naval honours gazetted on November 30, 1917, contained the following:

Distinguished Service Cross, Lt. T. B. McNabb, R.N.V.R.—In recognition of his gallantry in going overboard and securing a line to a drifting mine after attempts to sink it by gunfire had failed owing to a choppy sea and considerable swell, which made accurate shooting impossible.

That story was accompanied by another contained in a report from "Western waters of the English Channel," an indication of locality which was a reminder that though the grimmest and hardest of the mine-sweeping work was necessarily in North Sea waters, yet it was unendingly conducted wherever it was necessary to keep the trade routes clear. It was an instance which in every way was in keeping with the achievement of the lieutenant who swam out to the mine in half a gale, and, like that, it had the added glory of being purely voluntary work.

A flotilla of mine-sweepers was sweeping between two given points when two mines exploded in the sweep which was towed by the second pair of mine-sweeping trawlers in the flotilla. The wire parted, and one of the two trawlers hove in the "kite"—the contrivance employed to keep the sweep at the required depth.

When the "kite" had been hove short up to the rollers it was seen that a mine was foul of the wire, and had been hauled up against the trawler's side; and not only that, but the outline of another mine was visible just below the surface. This second mine was entangled in the sweeping-wire and was swirling in the eddy under the vessel's counter.

The situation was one of the most extreme peril and called for the greatest courage and promptness on the part of the officer in charge. Both were forthcoming. He ordered the trawler to be abandoned.

That was but the beginning of one of the dramas of the sweeping service, it was, so to speak, the train which fired the powder. The little vessel might well have been left to chance or fate—for one trawler lost from thousands could not matter much, so long as the crew were safe. But the senior officer in command of the mine-sweepers had no intention of letting the gallant little craft go in such a fashion—if she could be saved at all he was determined to preserve her, and in the right British way he led the volunteering, calling for a man to go with him.

An engineman—he was described as "the" engineman, and presumably belonged to the temporarily abandoned ship—responded to the call, and together they boarded the rolling craft which at any moment might be blown to pieces. Having reached her they set to work on their perilous task, and reckless of the risk they ran, cut the sweeping-wire and the "kite" wire, with the joyful result that the two mines fell clear without exploding, and they were towed clear of the spot by means of a rope which had been passed to another trawler.

This fine act stood in something like splendid isolation, for it was not a case of saving life; it was merely a matter of preserving a little ship. Quite apart from the courage shown, it might stand on record as a unique salvage deed.

Women had responded to the national call in vast numbers, particularly in relation to munition work; and in many parts of the country they did valuable work in keeping inshore fisheries busy. It was no new thing for women in certain regions to take a standing share in the industry, apart from the army of Scotch fisher girls and such bodies as the "flithers" women of the Flamborough and Filey districts; but it was a departure for wives and daughters to go out to sea and fish.

Deeds were performed in connection with the war which were worthy of being placed side by side with the achievement of Grace Darling, and such was the case of a girl of twenty to which attention was called in the House of Commons. This heroine was Miss Ella Trout, of Hall Sands, South Devon, who rescued some of the survivors of a torpedoed ship. She was out in her boat, with her cousin, a boy of ten, lifting her crab-pots, when she saw a cargo boat coming up from the westward. At that time she was just off Start Point. Just as she was watching the steamer she heard a terrible explosion and the ship vanished, showing that the torpedo had done its deadly work swiftly.

The girl had the sails up, but she lowered them at once, as the wind was in the wrong quarter for sailing to the scene of the disaster. She and the boy took an oar each and pulled hard to the spot, about three-quarters of a mile away. Having reached it, she saw several persons swimming about, and the first to be able to lay hands on was a negro who proved to be a fireman of the lost vessel. He and other men were keeping themselves afloat on some wreckage.

The negro was exhausted, but the girl managed to save him. Doubtless she and the boy would have saved others, but a motor boat came up and rescued the rest of the survivors. It was the fireman who told the girl that the steamboat had been torpedoed by a submarine. The case was so unusual that the circumstances were investigated by the Board of Trade, with a view to the girl's services being rewarded.

The Albert Medal was conferred upon two members of the Grimsby steam trawler *Exeter*, at Buckingham Palace, on November 14, 1917, for gallant acts. These men were Ernest Henry Outhouse, deckhand, formerly third hand, and William Weldrick, trimmer, formerly deckhand, both of the Trawler Section, Royal Naval Reserve.

The awards were made for one of those life-saving efforts, in circumstances of great danger, which had always marked the heroic deeds of trawlermen.

On November 20, 1916, the *ketch Frieda*, of London, was in a sinking state in the North Sea. She made signals of distress, and in prompt response to them the *Exeter* approached the spot and a small boat was launched under the command of the second hand and manned by Outhouse, Weldrick and two other men. The boat proceeded to the *ketch*, but was so much damaged by the heavy seas that she was forced to return to the trawler. The *Exeter* was then manoeuvred into a favourable position, and lines with bladders attached were thrown overboard. The *Frieda's* crew of three hands jumped into the water and two of them were hauled on board the trawler by means of the lines, the other man being drowned. Owing to the heavy seas which were running very considerable risk was incurred in rendering the services which saved two of the men from the *ketch*.

Prior to the presentation of the Albert Medal to Outhouse and

Weldrick medals had been awarded to the other men who went in the rescuing boat.

The king also presented the Albert Medal to Herbert Powley, a deckhand, who had shown great courage in connection with an explosion on board one of H.M. motor launches. The launch was lying alongside the jetty at a base when a violent explosion occurred and wrecked the after part of the vessel.

It became known that Sub-Lieutenant Charles W. Nash, R.N.V.R., was buried beneath the wreckage. Chief Alotor Mechanic Pooley and Deckhand Powley, who were on board their own vessel lying about fifty yards astern, hurried at once to the motor launch, which by this time was burning fiercely.

The flames were rapidly drawing near to the spot where the officer lay buried, and it was clear that there was a likelihood of the after petrol tanks exploding at any moment. Such an occurrence would have meant instant death to Powley and Pooley, but regardless of this terrible risk they jumped on board the little craft and succeeded in extricating Sub-Lieutenant Nash from beneath the wreckage and carrying him to the jetty.

The rescue was carried out just in time, for even as they were leaving the vessel the whole of the after part burst into flames and a delay of another thirty seconds would have meant that all three would have perished. Powley, who had gallantly led the way on to the burning motor launch, had to be sent to hospital, suffering from the effects of fumes.

This was an enterprise of exceptional peril and was carried out in the spirit of daring and self-sacrifice which had been so frequently displayed by the heroes to whom the Victoria Cross had been awarded.

Amongst the outstanding deeds of trawlers and drifters were the extraordinary performances of destroying enemy seaplanes. These acts were officially recorded in the summer of 1917. The first related to the bringing down of two seaplanes by a drifter. The details were necessarily brief, but they were enough to show how fine the achievement was. The vice-admiral at Dover reported that at about five o'clock on the morning of a Monday in June one of H.M. drifters, the *I.F.S.*, Lieutenant H. B. Bell Irving, R.N.V.R., in command, whilst on patrol duty, encountered five enemy seaplanes and engaged them.

One machine was destroyed, the pilot being rescued by another enemy machine. This machine was in turn attacked by the drifter and both pilots were taken prisoners, the machine being so badly damaged that it sank while being towed into harbour. The remaining three enemy seaplanes made good their escape. The *I.F.S.* was built in 1908 at Grimsby, and was registered and owned at Yarmouth. Amongst the officers upon whom decorations were conferred by the king at Buckingham Palace, on November 14, 1917, was Lieutenant Bell Irving, who received the Distinguished Service Cross and Bar.

The second achievement in connection with enemy seaplanes, which had become very active over the waters, was by an armed trawler, the announcement being made by the Admiralty on July 10. The statement merely intimated that the Commodore, Lowestoft, reported that at 8 p.m., on July, 9, H.M. armed trawler *Iceland*, Lieutenant P. Douglas, R.N.R., in command, destroyed two enemy seaplanes and brought four prisoners back into port. *The Times* correspondent at Lowestoft gave some interesting supplementary details. He said that the two seaplanes, carrying torpedoes, were bent on the destruction of craft in the North Sea. One of them came down, and, it was said, discharged a "torpedo" at a passing steamer. The weapon missed its mark, and by that time the patrol vessel had come within striking distance.

The seaplane, after missing its quarry, tried to rise, but there was a choppy sea on, and the waves swept over its planes, preventing it from getting off the water. While the machine was making these efforts, a well-directed shot from the patrol's gun smashed it and the seaplane began to settle in the water, with the two occupants struggling to get free from the wreckage.

The other seaplane swooped down to give help, but that machine also was smashed by gunfire. The two men from the first seaplane were rescued by another patrol boat, and subsequently the other two were picked up. One man was badly injured in the right foot.

As the second machine was still afloat attempts were made to secure it, but it broke in halves and gradually settled down. Parts of the wreckage, however, were picked up, and these, with the captured airmen, were landed at an East coast town. Later in the day they left by train, each prisoner with a guard in reserved compartments, the object of considerable interest to passengers and others who, having heard of their departure, had assembled to get a glance of the captives.

An interesting feature in comparing these two fine acts was that one of them was performed so early as five o'clock in the morning and the other so late as eight o'clock in the evening.

NORTH SEA TRAWLERS CONVERTED INTO MINE-SWEEPERS

SKIPPER WRIGHT, WHO DISCOVERED THE
"KONIGEN LUISE," A GERMAN MINE-LAYER, WHICH WAS
DESTROYED EARLY IN THE WAR.

CHAPTER 8

# "Submarine Billy"

Fishermen had got used to being drowned. Life-long experience had taught them the futility of trying to save themselves when once in the water; and most of them could not swim. They were to get used to worse things than being drowned, for that fate at least brought rest. In going to sea, however, in war-time the fisherman knew neither rest nor comfort. He was incessantly on the alert, constantly on the rack. If he escaped the mine there was the submarine; if he evaded underwater perils he was the prey of any prowling cruiser, destroyer or other enemy craft that might have temporary freedom on the seas; and if he kept clear of all these dangers, there was still the very serious chance of attack from the air by airship or aeroplane.

Through every one of these causes fishermen suffered heavy losses. In many instances the men did not live to tell the tale of their adventures; but there were survivors who gave details of happenings at sea which made the exploits of romance-writers almost feeble by comparison. It was not easy for the ordinary civilised person to believe that such iniquities could be practised, and some sort of faith was still put in German promises, some slender belief in German humanity prevailed until accumulated deeds of barbarism shattered the trust of even the most credulous and indulgent persons.

Amazing stories were told, tales that were incontestibly true, of men surviving one bad disaster only to survive a worse; and remarkable even amongst these was the narrative which follows. The teller, William Thomas Baker, a North Sea fisherman, living on the East coast, became known as "Submarine Billy" because of the affairs with which he was unwillingly associated. His experiences showed something of the price that had to be paid for fish in time of war. "Submarine Billy," who was seen as soon as he came ashore at the end of one of his trips in a beam-trawler, said:—

"It was nearly a year after the war began that I was fishing in the smack *Prospector*, about eighteen miles out, east-south-east of Lowestoft. By that time the war had made a lot of difference to fishermen and the North Sea fishing. Most of the ordinary fishermen, both fleeters and single-boaters, had joined up for mine-sweeping and patrolling, and war work in other ways, and those who went to sea to fish were either men over fighting age, like myself, or boys.

"As everybody knows now, immense numbers of steam trawlers and drifters had been taken over as Government boats, and many of the old beam-trawlers had got a new lease of life. These had to be contented with short-handed crews, and the *Prospector*, instead of carrying five hands, had only four—the skipper, the second hand (mate, myself), the third hand, and the cook, who did plenty besides cooking.

"It was hard and racking work all the time, because the Germans reckoned that we were fair game for their submarines. A few of these craft managed to show themselves from time to time and attack poor little fishing vessels and fishermen who were absolutely unable to help themselves. There's many a fisherman suffering cruelly now in German prison camps, having lost everything he possessed, besides his liberty, and for doing nothing worse than going to sea to make a living and help to keep his country supplied with food. The North Sea is a big stretch of water, and even the British Navy can't be all over it and everywhere at one time; so that sometimes the Germans show their noses, but not for long, and always in a state of terror.

"On the morning of August 10, 1915, I was on deck. The weather was very calm, so we hadn't our gear down. It was just before noon, and I was looking round pretty sharply, as you do in these days at sea, when I saw a German submarine quite close to us. He must have seen us through his periscope and come to the surface, and there he was awash, like some ugly brute looking for prey. There was no mistaking him—I knew at once what he was, for I had been fifteen years in the Royal Naval Reserve.

"There were several other smacks about, with beam-trawls, like ours, and as completely defenceless as we were. There wasn't a ghost of a chance of doing anything against such an enemy as this—we just had to wait and see what happened. We hadn't long to wait.

"Almost as soon as I had spotted the submarine he came towards us, and the commander, as I took him to be, who was standing on the platform, shouted to us in quite good English, 'I will give you five minutes to leave your ship!'

"We chucked the boat out and got into it. We didn't bother to get our clothing or anything; we daren't, and there wasn't time. We were ordered to go to the submarine, and we pulled to her.

"When we got alongside three of our fellows scrambled on board, leaving me in the boat, where I was joined by two German sailors who carried bombs in their hands. There were two bombs, one rather like a fair-sized, round, fancy flower-pot, and the other bigger, and jug-shaped, with a handle for carrying. These two men couldn't speak English—at any rate, they didn't say anything to me, and I said nothing to them. They had their orders, and carried them out.

"The German commander said to me, 'Take these two men back to the smack.'

"As soon as we were alongside the smack the boat was made fast, and the Germans got on board and went below with their bombs.

"By this time the submarine had come up, on the weather side, quite close to the smack, and the commander, who was greatly excited and seemed terribly nervous about British warships, shouted, 'Hurry up! Hurry up!' and I can tell you no time was lost by anybody.

"The Germans weren't long below. They planted their bombs and then rushed up on deck and jumped back into the boat, and I sculled to the submarine.

"A very strange little thing happened while all this was going on.

"The German commander said to our third hand, 'I knew you in Yarmouth. I kept a shop in Millgate Street. They used to call me Peter.'

"The third hand said afterwards that he didn't remember the German at all; but what he said may have been true, and he may have been one of the Germans who lived in England and waited for the war to come.

"About a quarter of an hour after we left the smack there was a terrific explosion; the deck split up, there was a lot of fire and smoke, she began to sink, and in about eight minutes she had gone altogether. Our floating home and everything in it went to the bottom, which is just about the same as a home ashore being destroyed with everything it contains.

"The Germans lost no time over their job. While this was going on our other three chaps had been ordered back into the boat, and we were told to go to another smack which was not far away—the *Ben Nevis*. This smack had been spared so that she could take on board the crews of vessels that were bombed.

"Then the Germans set to work to destroy, as fast as they could, the smacks that were about, one after the other, leaving one or two to bring the crews away. The Germans at that time did not even try to take anything away for themselves, such as brass and copper; they just bombed and sank the smacks. It was a cowardly and cruel thing to do, for we hadn't a bullet or weapon of any sort amongst us, and we had absolutely nothing to do with the war.

"Another smack near us, the *Venture*, was blown up, and her crew were put on board the *Ben Nevis*, so that she had three crews on board, and there we all were crowded, fairly upset, not knowing what was going to happen next. We had made our little boat fast astern as soon as we got on board the *Ben Nevis*.

"We spent a wearying night, and very thankful we were when the morning came. Luckily, a patrolboat, the *Retriever*, came up and pulled us inshore, to the westward, and later a big mine-sweeper brought us into Lowestoft. It was good to be ashore again, after such a shaking. But I was soon to have a far worse experience than the bombing of the *Prospector*.

"I was in no hurry to go back to sea; but a man has to live, so after exactly a month ashore I shipped as third hand on board the *Boy Ernie*, and went trawling again.

"On Friday, September 10, 1915, at five minutes to eight o'clock, when we were just outside the Long Shoal, I was standing by the cabin hoodway, threading a needle of black twine. We hadn't shot the gear, as we had lost our trawl through fouling a wreck, and we had bent a new trawl.

"We were getting ready to shoot, and as I filled the needle I looked around, being pretty suspicious.

"Suddenly, about half a mile away, I saw two submarines, and I had no sooner spied them than one of them began to fire on us.

"'Skipper,' I said, ' there's two German submarines.'

"The skipper looked and said, 'No, they're English.'

"'No, they're not,' I said. 'Do you mean to say that if they were English they'd fire on fishing smacks? Of course, they wouldn't. They're Germans.' And so they were, and as soon as they'd come up they'd begun to fire on us.

"It was very heavy and deliberate fire. The shots, three-pounders, were coming on deck and going through the sails. One shell came along, and I just stepped aside, like this, and it missed me and went through the bulwarks. The shots went right through the bulwarks, which, of course, are not very thick, and they were going through all the sails, ripping holes in them.

"I said to the skipper, 'It's time we were getting the boat out.'

"The skipper said, 'All right,' and we threw her overboard—she was on deck—pulled her alongside by the painter, and tumbled into her as hard as we could. This was on the lee side, away from the firing.

"There were no other craft in sight, only a 'Dutch' sailing vessel—at any rate, she was pretending to be Dutch, but, as a matter of fact, she was feeding the submarines with petrol.

"I started sculling the boat away from the smack, and we got about twenty yards astern very quickly, all the time under fire; but the Germans were not content with firing shells at a helpless craft—they now turned a machine-gun on to defenceless fishermen who were adrift in a boat on the open sea.

"There was amongst us a little boy—William Collins, they called him, only fourteen years and a half old. His mother was a widow, and he had four little brothers and sisters, so that the two or three shillings a week he earned was a help to her. Being such a little chap he was naturally scared at such a terrible business, and he was crying.

"'Get into the bottom of the boat, Billy,' I said. 'You'll be safer there.' And he did. He lay there, under the thwart, and I sat over him, protecting him as best I could.

"The boat was getting actually riddled by the machine-gun fire—later on it was seen how she had been peppered and holed, so that it was wonderful she kept afloat—and before I knew what was happening I was struck by a bullet on the right thigh, and began to bleed dreadfully.

"I knew no more at the time than that I had been hurt in some way, but as a matter of fact I had been struck by a bullet, which passed through the right thigh and would have gone through the left if it had not been stopped by this round steel tobacco-box, which was full of tobacco, and was at the bottom of a deep pocket, which had worked round to the inside of the leg. The hard metal turned the bullet aside, and instead of going through my left thigh it glanced off and went somewhere else—either into the boat or the sea.

"I was the only one in the boat to be struck or hurt—and I'm glad to say it.

"The Germans went on bombarding the smack and smashing her

up, and she was finished off with bombs. She was blown to pieces, and went down with all her sails set, a pitiful spectacle. This was the work of one of the two submarines—while she was sinking the smack the other was firing on us.

"When they had done their work both the submarines slunk down again into the depths of the sea.

"For six hours and a half we were in that small boat, and I never expected to do anything but bleed to death. I managed to stanch the bleeding a bit, however, somehow, and when we were picked up—as we were by a big mine-sweeper—I was soon put to rights. They washed my wound and bound it up. They did all they could for me, every man of them—and they didn't forget little Billy either.

"While they were washing and bandaging me, a wireless message was sent to Yarmouth, where it was known that a smack's crew had been picked up, one of them being severely wounded.

"When I was brought in I was too bad for them to shift me except on a stretcher, and so I was put into one and taken in a naval motor car to Yarmouth Hospital. That was at seven o'clock in the evening, nearly twelve hours after I had first seen the two submarines. At nine I was operated on, and then I was in hospital for a month.

"Little Billy was a splendid chap. He had been badly scared, but he pulled up, and in two or three days went to sea again.

"I was ashore for twenty weeks, and then I was forced to go to sea again, because I couldn't get anything to do. I didn't want to go—I was thoroughly shattered, and had pretty well gone to pieces. I had suffered terribly, especially at night, when often enough I would go through the whole of the bombing and firing again—just as real, it seemed, as the actual performance.

"Being unable to get anything to do ashore, I went to the west-ward to help to bring a ship home that had been ashore. Then I was in a tosher for three weeks—a tosher is a small three-hand craft, rigged just the same as a big smack—and after that I went fishing in the smack Waverley, and got about sixteen miles off Cromer.

"By this time I had become known as 'Submarine Billy,' owing to my adventures with the Germans at sea, and very soon the nickname fitted me better than ever.

"I was getting used to German submarines, so I wasn't much surprised, though I wasn't pleased or happy, when, after breakfast on the morning of July 17, 1916, I saw another German submarine, and felt pretty certain that it was all up with us again.

"My nerves had been broken altogether by the earlier experiences, and I was badly upset now when the Germans began to fire on the *Waverley*. This we soon took to be a warning to leave the smack—and we acted on it. Again our gear was up, because of the calm weather, so that we were absolutely helpless; we had not even the bit of a chance of escaping which a breeze might have given us.

"The vessel was perfectly still, so that it was easy to get the boat overboard through the gangway. We should have done that even if the commander had not shouted through a megaphone: 'You have got to leave your ship!' That seemed to be the usual order with them.

"As soon as our little boat was afloat we jumped into her and pulled away from the vessel, leaving everything we possessed.

"Firing was going on all the time, but we were not hit.

"A very strange thing soon happened. The submarine came up alongside the little boat, and the commander, who could speak very good English, astonished us by saying that he was very sorry for what he was doing; but he could not help himself—he was forced to do it. He said, 'I was in the P. & O. service for seven years, and the English people treated me very well.' He was honest and he was certainly a gentleman.

"This time the Germans helped themselves to fish, food, flour, and other things of ours before putting bombs on board the smack and blowing her up. She went just as the other two had gone—my third floating home to be blown up by the Germans.

"Again we were left to it in a little open boat at sea, and for nearly five hours we were cruising about, doing our best to get to shore. We pulled into Hasborough Roads, and then H.M.S. *Halcyon* picked us up, and we were aboard her all that night and next day, chasing the submarine and a Dutch craft; but we hadn't the luck to catch them, and I was sent ashore.

"I had had my third escape from the Germans, and was thankful to be ashore again. When my wife met me she said, 'Haven't you brought a bit of fish home?'

"My brother-in-law, who was present, and had heard about my last adventure, chimed in with, 'You may think yourself lucky he's home at all—he's been blown up again.'

"The name 'Submarine Billy' had stuck to me; but next time I went to sea I was to have a change.

"After being ashore only two weeks I went trawling again—for I have to live. That was the only reason for my going out once more in a smack. This time I was second hand in the *Francis Roberts*.

"At about half-past one in the morning of July 31 I was on watch, the rest of the crew being below. There was a thick fog over the water, but it was lovely and bright up aloft and the stars were out.

"All at once I heard a sound that you never mistake—the whir of an airship's propellers.

"There were some steam trawlers about, and as soon as they heard the noise they began to blow their whistles, to warn the smacks to look out as sharp as they could. There was a terrific commotion and tremendous excitement; then there were heavy explosions, for the crew of the airship, which was a Zeppelin, were dropping bombs. I don't think they could see the trawlers, owing to the fog; but they could hear the whistles going, and hoped to get the vessels.

"In some ways this was a worse experience than the rest, for it was impossible to do anything, and any instant a bomb might strike us and simply wipe us out. I couldn't leave the deck, as my duty kept me there, so, unnerving though it was, I watched bombs exploding in the air, and heard others bursting, though I could not see them owing to the fog. It was horrible to listen to them. I was shaking like a leaf, and so, I think, would most men in the same position. I could not possibly help it, after what I had been through.

"It mercifully happened that no vessel was hit, and all the bombs were dropped in vain, so far as damage went; but as for me, I was poisoned by the awful fumes of a bomb which burst not far above me.

"The airship's crew could not see us; but the bomb only just cleared our smack, exploding before it touched the water. Being on deck I got the full force of the fumes, while the rest of the crew, being below, were lucky enough to escape.

"Some of the other trawlers cut their gear and went away for home, and we got into the land as quickly as we could—thankful that there was just wind enough for that. The first craft we spoke was the *Dragoon*. We asked if they had seen a Zepp., and they said, 'Yes, one passed just over the topmast!' So that little craft had a very narrow escape.

"By this time the fog had lifted and the weather was clear—we owed our wonderful preservation to being hidden. It isn't often you can speak well of a North Sea fog.

"After getting home I was lying on the couch for nine days, with one eye quite closed. The poison gas had turned me as yellow as saffron, and I suffered cruelly. All the time, of course, I hadn't a penny coming in, and I could get no help from any fund; but at last the Deep

Sea Mission set me up, and with a heavy heart I went to sea again, joining the *Glory*, this time as third hand.

"I fully expected that something would happen again, and I was on the rack all the time; but, you see, she's safely home again, after a week's trip."

THE SKIPPER OF A MINE-SWEEPER IN THE WHEELHOUSE.

CHAPTER 9

# Armed Trawlers and Salvage

Very often, in the days before the war, steam trawlers did uncommonly brave and skilful salvage work. These warriors of the storms were here, there and everywhere upon the home and distant waters, and if such a desirable thing as a lame duck was seen that prize was mercifully swooped down upon and, if tenacity and pluck could get it into port, the helpless vessel was towed or otherwise taken into the sheltering haven.

First of all things in the mind of the deep sea fisherman was the wish to save his fellow-mortals, for he knew so well what it meant to be the victim of the gales and fogs and accidents. In many cases the matter began and ended there, and fine acts were never more than orally recorded, to become legendary in fleets and fishing ports.

There was much of the spirit of a lift-on-the-way shown, much of the display of the brotherhood of the sea; succour and salvation by men who knew that in the hour of their own extremity the helping hand would be stretched forth even as their own had been. But there was always the knowledge that if important salvage work were successfully accomplished there would be an appropriate reward, and that the recompense might well be considerable.

These deeds were done with even greater *éclat* after the war broke out than before hostilities began, for to the ordinary perils of the sea were added the graver dangers of the mine and submarine and the isolated enemy cruiser, destroyer or raider that might have had the brief good fortune to elude the Allied navies.

Such a performance was to the credit of a steamboat which was trawling in the Irish Sea early in 1915. The trawler sighted a powerful new tug which was in distress through a breakdown of her machinery. A whole gale was blowing and very heavy seas were running, and the task of even attempting salvage was difficult and dangerous. But the skipper and his crew set to work in the old North Sea style, bringing to the Western waters the experience of a lifetime on the Eastern area. After many hard efforts and repeated failures a hawser was made fast to the tug, and the rousing work of towing began; but a promising start had an early setback in the parting of the hawser, and the helpless tug swung off and wallowed in the deeps.

Then came one of those long contests of dodging and daring which are common to achievements of this sort in wild weather; and as the result of the united efforts of men who badly wanted to be saved and of those who longed to succour them, a second hawser was made fast, a success which was quickly followed by a second snap and a more perilous position for the helpless tug.

The stern fight went on, a fight which had become first of all a question of saving fellow-creatures who were almost at the last extremity.

For the third time, and, as it proved, the last time, a hawser was made fast, and with this fresh good start, and the combined skill and seamanship of the trawlerman and the tugman both vessels safely reached port.

This was an exceptionally creditable piece of work, and there was little doubt that if it had not been for the persistent efforts of the fishermen the tug would have been lost with all hands.

In the special circumstances the case was one of salvage, and it seemed likely that the courts would have to settle the matter, but finally an arrangement was made without unduly calling in the law; but more than two years passed before the trawlermen, who had done so well, received the proper acknowledgment of their valuable services.

Not long after that splendid performance on the Irish Sea the fishing vessel, a very fine example of her class, manned by a fittingly fine skipper and crew, was taken over by the Admiralty; the skipper was absorbed in the Navy, and his crew also became members of the great army of sweepers and patrollers.

The war raised many important questions of salvage law, and cases that were heard in the courts had features of special interest, while it was through their medium that for the first time the public became acquainted with the details of numerous gallant acts at sea.

Amongst these instances was that of a Swedish steamer which was attacked by a German submarine, and a trawler's claim for salvage arose. The action was heard in the Probate, Divorce and Admiralty

Division, before Mr. Justice Hill and the Elder Brethren of the Trinity House, and a report of the case appeared in *The Times* on August 1, 1917.

The circumstances of the case were these:—On January i, 1917, the *Carrie*, a Swedish steamship, was attacked by a German submarine when she was about 20 miles to the south of the Wolf Rock lighthouse. She was on a voyage from Glasgow to Nantes with a cargo of munitions for the French Government. In obedience to the orders of the German officer the crew of the *Carrie* took to the boats. A little later H.M. armed trawlers *Fusilier* and *Kinaldie* arrived and picked up the crew. In the meantime the submarine had disappeared without sinking the *Carrie*. As her crew refused to return to her, she was towed by the trawlers into Falmouth. The action was brought by the commanders, officers and crews of the *Fusilier* and *Kinaldie* against the owners of the *Carrie*. The defendants denied that salvage was due, contending that the vessel was merely saved from war risks, and that there was a duty on His Majesty's ships to save the cargo, which was the property of an Allied Government; and the saving of the ship was a mere incident in the saving of the cargo.

In delivering a considered judgement, Mr. Justice Hill said:—

"Both vessels were in the service of His Majesty and therefore the services of the ships as instruments of salvage were gratuitous. The only question is what were the personal services of the plaintiffs, and were they salvage services, and, if they were, what is a proper award? Undoubtedly the trawlers saved the *Carrie* from a position of peril and brought her in safety into Falmouth; but the circumstances have to be considered.

"The plaintiffs say that the submarine submerged on sighting the trawlers. The trawlers claim no merit in this. They had had a report of a submarine and were searching for it when they sighted the *Carrie*. On coming up Lieutenant Massey, who was in command, told the master to return to the *Carrie* and said that the trawlers would escort him to Ushant. The crew were unwilling and the master refused to return. The *Kinaldie* took the crew out of the boats and throughout the night the two trawlers patrolled about the *Carrie*. So far there is no dispute. As to what happened on the following morning there is a complete contradiction of evidence. The evidence of the master and others of the crew is that they asked to be allowed to return to the ship and continue their voyage, and that permission was refused. The evidence from the trawlers is that the master of the *Carrie* was urged to return to his ship with his crew and that he refused. Had the defendants' evidence been true it would have reflected greatly upon those in charge of the trawlers; but it is not true.

"I have heard and seen the witnesses and considered the documents, and I have no hesitation in arriving at the conclusion that the master and crew of the *Carrie* refused to return to the ship. I do not blame them. They had been ordered by the enemy to quit the ship; they had a cargo on board which made them peculiarly liable to attack, and if the submarine again found them on board and on their way to France they would have got very short shrift. I am satisfied that these considerations and their experiences of the day before had unnerved the master and made him only too glad to leave himself and the *Carrie* to the care of the trawlers.

"The *Fusilier* then put out her boat and sent the second hand and three men on board the *Carrie*—with the swell, and with no one on board the *Carrie*, it was naturally a work of some risk to get on board—and it was found that the fires had burnt out and there was no steam in the *Carrie's* engines. A hawser was passed and the *Fusilier* made fast. About 8 o'clock the *Fusilier* began to tow, with the *Kinaldie* accompanying as escort. About 9 o'clock the hawser parted and the *Kinaldie* made fast and began to tow about 9.45, with the *Fusilier* accompanying as escort. At 3.15, outside Falmouth, the *Fusilier* also made fast to assist to steer. At 5 o'clock the *Carrie* was brought to a safe anchorage in Falmouth Harbour.

"The case would be a simple one but for the contention of the defendants that the plaintiffs , being the commanders, officers, and crews of King's ships, are not entitled to any salvage against the Swedish ship, because she was carrying cargo for the French Government. The contention is that the plaintiffs were under a duty to save the property of an Allied Government, and the saving of the ship was a mere incident in the saving of the cargo. It is also said that the saving was not from maritime, but from war perils.

"I have already found that the crew refused to return to their ship. It is clear therefore that the saving was not only from submarine attack but also from maritime perils. But for the assistance of the plaintiffs the *Carrie* would have been left in the open sea with no one on board. The plaintiffs brought her into port. No doubt the ship was being saved from maritime perils. She was also saved from enemy attack; but she was not saved only from enemy attack.

"The question is whether the plaintiffs are entitled to salvage for saving the ship from maritime perils, and perhaps also whether the Court ought to take into account the saving from war perils. Assuming that the cargo was the property of the French Government, and assuming also that it is the duty of the officers and crews of King's ships to protect the property of Allied Governments, I do not think that that makes the service *qua* the neutral ship any less a salvage service. . . . Assuming that the plaintiffs were under a duty to the cargo, I think that does not prevent their being salvors of the ship.

"They have in fact saved the ship to the Swedish owners. Whatever was their duty to their own country or to France, they were under no duty to the Swedish owners to save the Swedish ship. They are therefore entitled to claim as salvors in respect of the ship, and I have not to consider whether they are entitled to claim as salvors in respect of the cargo. The saving of the Swedish ship being by the plaintiffs a salvage service, I see no reason in principle why the whole risks of the salved property, war risks as well as maritime, are not to be taken into account in estimating the value of the service to the salved property. In this case I shall take the whole risks into account. . . .

"The award which I think ought to be made is an award of £750. If it is desired that I should apportion that sum, then I give £375 to the officers and crews of each of the plaintiffs' ships."

The circumstances which were made known in the judgment showed that the salvage of the Swedish ship was an undertaking of great danger and that the crews of the armed trawlers followed a fine and courageous lead. They added to the high character of their achievement the glory of sending a German submarine back to the depths, and they showed how very greatly armed trawlers were helping the bigger vessels of the Navy in keeping the command of the sea. The award was small, but it was an acknowledgment of the dangerous duty which these two little steamboats had performed.

On the day on which he gave judgement in the *Carrie* case, Mr. Justice Hill awarded £12,280 to various vessels in connection with the salvage of the P. & O. steamer *Poena* in December, 1917. Amongst these vessels were the armed trawlers *Sheldan, Offa II.* and *Cedar*. On December 6 the *Poona*, when off Beachy Head, on a voyage from London to Calcutta with general cargo and a crew of 121 hands, struck a mine and received great damage. She immediately began to go down rapidly by the head, with a list to starboard. Fortunately the weather was fine.

All hands were called on deck, the engines were stopped, the boats were lowered, S.O.S. signals were sent out, and all hands took to the boats; but afterwards the master, first, second, third officers, chief engineer, three able seamen and six lascars returned on board, and eventually the *Poona* was towed first to Stokes Bay and then into dock at Portsmouth. Her total value was £564,500—the ship £132,500 and the cargo £432,000. To each of the three armed trawlers the judge awarded £150.

These cases of salvage by armed trawlers emphasize two important facts, first the great value of these handy little vessels in helping to save for the Allies such cargoes as the *Carrie* and the *Poona* carried, and secondly their ubiquity. It was almost impossible for a nautical event of any sort to happen during the war without some part, great or small, being played by a steam trawler or drifter engaged in mine-sweeping, patrolling or fishing.

Some consolation and comfort were given to commanders and crews of armed trawlers in the opportunities they had of earning salvage money, as a set-off against the large sums which crews of vessels fishing in the ordinary way were known to be making.

It became usual, in notices issued by the Department of the Accountant-General of the Navy of intended distribution of salvage awards to find the inclusion of H.M. trawlers. Sometimes one vessel would be named, but often several were mentioned, and in one list no fewer than six were named in connection with the salvage of the steamship *Formosa*. These were H.M. trawlers *Nodzu, Spider, Evangel, King Erik, Thunderstone* and *Esher*. An interesting circumstance was that the announcement of the intended distribution of the award was made exactly two years from the date of the salvage itself, the *Formosa* being salved on November 14, 1915, and the announcement made public on November 14, 1917.

Long delays in settlements and awards were inevitable owing to the war and the exceptional difficulties arising out of hostilities, and it necessarily happened that men who had done such splendid service did not live to enjoy their merited reward. Substantial sums went to owners and skippers in some cases of salvage, but these extras were far below the amounts of the exceptional earnings of men who were following the ordinary fishing industry.

Amongst the cases relating to mine-sweepers and fishermen which from time to time came into courts of law was one of an interesting nature regarding an insurance policy which did not show the company concerned in a very favourable light.

A fisherman had insured his life by a policy dated November 14, 1914. He expected to go mine-sweeping, but while waiting to do so he disappeared, and it was supposed that he had fallen overboard. The executrix claimed to recover the amount due under the policy, but the company refused to pay, alleging that the fisherman had made misrepresentations on his proposal form and had withheld material information. The misrepresentations and concealment alleged were a statement that the policy was for his own benefit, and a statement that he was a fisherman, whereas, in fact, besides being a fisherman he was a member of the Royal Naval Reserve, and at the time of making the proposal he had been called up for service.

The case was originally heard by a county court judge, who decided that there was no evidence that the agent who took the proposal ever communicated the facts to the company before the issue of the policy, and he therefore held that the policy was void *ab initio* and that the receipt of premiums by the superintendent after the issue of the policy did not bind the company. He therefore gave judgement for the company.

The matter was not allowed to rest at that stage. The plaintiff appealed against the decision of the county court judge and the case came before Mr. Justice Lawrence and Mr. Justice Atkin.

Both these judges delivered judgment to the same effect, holding that the county court judge had come to a wrong conclusion; and they allowed the appeal. Mr. Justice Lawrence said that the assured was a fisherman, as stated on the form, but he was also called up in the Royal Naval Reserve, a fact which was not stated on the form, and the question was whether his having been called up without the statement of that fact vitiated the policy. In his opinion it did not. True, there was a provision on the form saying that omission or concealment of material facts would render the policy void.

But the defendants made these contracts with ignorant people, and had superintendents and district managers, who supervised the local agents and communicated information to the head office; and here the district manager was told that the fisherman was in the Naval Reserve, and it was only reasonable to suppose that telling the manager was equivalent to telling the head office. Communications made to such a person would be assumed by any reasonable assured person to be communicated to the head office. The manager had no power to make a new contract, but the old contract subsisted, and any objection that might have been taken was waived by the subsequent receipt of premiums.

Allowing this particular appeal was a satisfactory development of a case in which a powerful company had by no means shown generous treatment of a man who had undertaken perilous work for his country' and had also wisely done his best to make some provision for those who were dependent on him.

As a set-off against this particular case there were not wanting examples of insurance companies which acted very liberally in the cases of mine sweepers and fishermen who had been lost at sea.

# CHAPTER 10

# An Adventure With German Pirates

The submarine warfare on fishing vessels varied strangely in intensity. The Germans had deliberately avowed their determination to spare no effort to drive these vessels from the sea, and their attacks were marked by unmitigated ruthlessness and almost incredible savagery. At one particular period, August, 1916, there was an extraordinarily ferocious outbreak on the part of the Germans. On the night of August 3 no fewer than eight fishing boats, most of them small motor herring drifters, were destroyed off the North East coast by a German submarine. Some of the crews were landed in the Tyne, and stories were told which showed how deliberately the work of havoc had been planned and carried out.

At this period also other vessels, steam trawlers and drifters, were destroyed, in many instances sinking with their valuable cargoes of fish. The Germans before destroying some of the vessels, which they did by placing bombs on board, plundered the craft, making a particular point of looting the food and all the metal fittings. It was noticeable that in carrying out this work of destruction most of the Germans were extremely nervous and intensely apprehensive of the sudden appearance of some British war vessel from whose vengeance they could not hope to escape.

A clear insight into the methods of German submarine warfare at this period was given by a Scotch skipper who had fallen into the pirates' power and had the good fortune to escape. The narrator was Mr. David Stewart, and his vessel was the *Jane Stewart*, of Cockenzie. The scene described by the skipper was just such a one as might have been observed in the higher parts of the North Sea before the war, when the herring fishery was being carried down towards the Yarmouth area. The *Jane Stewart* was a fine, practically new craft of a type which

A MINE-SWEEPER DAMAGED BY STRIKING A MINE

had proved very successful, both as a fisher and commercially. She was fitted with a powerful motor, a means of propulsion which had stood many a craft in good stead in bad weather and danger-zones. She was surrounded by a large fleet of fishing vessels, which had their drift-nets out, their lights showing, and lookout men on duty—and lookout men in those times and places understood to the full the stern need of incessant watchfulness. The details of what happened on the night of August 3, 1916, were told by the skipper to a representative of *The Scotsman*, in which newspaper they were published.

The night was exceptionally calm—it was spoken of as one of the calmest nights that the fishermen had ever known at sea. Things on board the *Jane Stewart* went well until midnight, then the lookout man called to the skipper, and said he had heard an explosion in the distance and suspected that a submarine was at work.

The sinister warning was not to be neglected for an instant—there was a tense time of listening, and the practised ears of the skipper and the crew caught sounds which sounded like directions for casting off ropes. These sounds, it was judged, came from the *Volunteer*, a Musselburgh boat, with an English crew, which was about half-a-mile away. Satisfied as to the nature of the warning, the skipper did not hesitate—he ordered the motor to be started and the nets to be abandoned. Almost immediately there was a second explosion and the lights of the *Volunteer* disappeared, and it was obvious that the vessel had been destroyed by a torpedo.

Such a swift onslaught on an entirely defenceless fleet of fishing vessels could have but one effect, and that was to spread alarm amongst the crews and make them take the only course open to them, and that was to seek safety in flight. Most of the steam drifters cut their nets adrift and steamed their hardest for harbour, and as it was impossible for one submarine to deal with all of them, as the Germans undoubtedly would have liked, most of the vessels, with the help that night gave them, found refuge in port.

Meanwhile it was clear that there was no hope of the *Jane Stewart* sharing this good fortune, for before she could get under way a submarine was rapidly approaching her. For a moment or two the skipper felt sure that the enemy craft meant to ram the drifter and cut her in two, for she was going straight at the helpless vessel; but just in time, as he expressed it, "she stopped like a train, and her bow came round until it was touching well forward."

The events that quickly followed showed how carefully planned the Germans' programme was, and indicated a close acquaintance with this particular form of cowardly attack and ruthless destruction. The vivid picture which the skipper drew did not tend to create a favourable impression of the men who did the dirty work of the German Navy. The officer in command was a "strapping fellow of about twenty-six years of age," and the skipper declared that there was not a man of the submarine crew who was under six feet in height. These heroes, undisturbed except by horrifying visions of the possible swoop of men of the British Navy hurried to complete their task.

No time was given for the drifter's crew to take away their belongings—and this was one of the minor but serious hardships which the Germans imposed, for it frequently happened in the fishing industry that when a man lost his personal possessions he lost his all.

The situation was bad, but it was relieved by one of those incidents which, though supposed to be particularly Scottish in character, are peculiarly associated with the fishing fraternity. The oldest member of the crew, a man named Hastie, of Cockenzie, was in his bunk when the Germans boarded the little drifter to destroy her. Hastie had an unusual stock of clothing on board, to see him through the ten weeks' fishing season, of which the vessel had completed about half. The garments were a treasured property, and all the more valued because they included a Sunday suit, which was held in readiness for wearing when, in due course. North Shields was reached. Hastie had not time even to put on his boots; but determined not to part lightly from his belongings he went to the forecastle and there found the gallant German officer in the forecastle, placing a bomb.

As soon as he saw Hastie the officer caught him by the shoulders, turned him sharply round, and in perfect English said, "You get on top!"

There was no help for it. The *Jane Stewart* was doomed, and it was not possible to tell what the ultimate fate of her crew might be. Their present case was bad enough, for they were ordered to go on board the submarine, and this they did, the task of reaching the upper part being difficult.

The drifter's crew were forced to crawl along the narrow ridge of the deck of the German vessel until they reached the platform amidships.

Having done this the skipper was confronted with the truly piratical spectacle of four huge Germans on either side of the platform. This guard in itself would have been enough to awe any helpless and imprisoned crew in a craft so strange; but the Germans did not take risks, and accordingly each of the eight held a big revolver ready for use, and from each man's belt hung a glittering axe.

The captives were ordered to go to the after part of the submarine, and they obeyed, but not without difficulty as it was dark and they discovered that the crews of two other destroyed fishing vessels were on board, making a score of fishermen in all. The skipper crouched beneath a powerful gun which the submarine carried on her deck.

An order was now given to cast off the lashings, but in the night there arose the cry, "Are you going to leave me behind?"

It was soon found that this appeal came from Hastie, who, still hoping for the salvation of his clothing, had remained on board the drifter.

Some spasm of humanity apparently possessed one of the Germans, who, like so many of his fellows operating in these submarines, understood English well, and he replied, "No, daddy!" There was something of a commotion, resulting in the sprawling of Hastie on the deck of the submarine and the bruising of his legs.

The skipper did the good service of carefully examining all that he could see on board the submarine, noticing, amongst other details, the height and position of the conning-tower, the calibre of the gun and the apparent dimensions of the deck. He observed that the commander was in the conning-tower and that during the whole of the time the skipper was on board, about an hour and a quarter, he gave orders to the crew. Three men were beside him, with large glasses, with which they continuously swept the sea, obviously keenly watchful for any sign of a British war vessel.

The submarine began to move off, gaining speed, and ultimately travelling at the rate of seventeen or eighteen knots an hour. In the meantime the officer who had boarded the drifter joined the skipper and closely questioned him concerning the other vessels. He asked whether any of the lights that were visible were from the coast, and was told that they were the lights of fishing-vessels.

"Are there any trawlers amongst them?" asked the German.

The skipper replied that there were none.

"Did any of the fishing vessels carry a gun?" continued this inquisitive Teuton, doubtless with a somewhat quickened beating of his brave heart. His fear on that important point having been set at rest another question indicating trepidation was put—When had the skipper last seen a war vessel? Not since he left the Tyne, the skipper answered.

These replies seemed to reassure the agitated German, who then, with more composure, shared in the acceptable task of giving close attention to another helpless vessel which they were approaching.

The skipper of the *Jane Stewart* was now informed that he and his companions were to be put on board this vessel. That intention, however, was frustrated in an unexpected fashion, for the skipper of the fishing vessel, rightly distrusting such an enemy, put out his lights with the object of protecting himself as best he could. But the submarine got alongside and her commander demanded to know why the lights had been extinguished. All that could be indicated by way of answer was that the crew of the boat had no wish to draw the close attention of the enemy.

The German law of "frightfulness" came into instant operation, and the little craft, which was to have been spared for the purpose of receiving men who could not be accommodated on board the submarine, was destroyed by bombs, her own crew being added to the crowd of fishermen already captives, raising the number to about thirty.

These helpless fishers were now in a position of the gravest peril, and there was not a man amongst them who did not realise this fact, for the Germans were intensely apprehensive of the appearance of a British war vessel and the prisoners knew perfectly well what their fate would be in such an event—the submarine would seek her own safety and leave them to drown, or at least to take their precarious chance of salvation from one of the few boats which were left afloat.

As it mercifully happened, the submarine in this respect was not troubled and she carried on and completed her work of destruction. Finally the fishermen were put on board a small vessel which had been spared and were left to themselves. Before the men were allowed to leave the submarine they were definitely directed as to what they should do, the spokesman being the officer who had boarded the *Jane Stewart* and had done most of the talking.

By way of emphasising his remarks, the German placed his arm round the skipper's shoulder—a contact which could not have been very acceptable—and spoke close to his ear.

It was insisted that the remaining fishing vessels should keep their lights burning until daylight, and the fact was emphasised that failure to obey this order would bring upon the offenders the prompt vengeance of the submarine. That this threat would have been instantly and ruthlessly carried out was unquestionable, for after putting the men on board the little vessel the submarine went away and proceeded to destroy other craft.

The crews who had been forced to take temporary refuge on the deck of the submarine had no food with them, and on board the craft to which they had been transferred there was little to be had; but there was, at any rate, the hopeful prospect of soon reaching port and finding help, security and comfort.

This welcome finish duly came to an adventure of an uncommonly dangerous nature, for it was only by sheer luck that a large number of the fishermen did not lose their lives. In several cases the crews were sent adrift in their little boats, some finding refuge at last in the surviving fishing vessels, which were already overcrowded, and some being picked up by a patrol boat.

The material loss as the result of this night's raid by a German submarine was great and seriously affected individuals. In the case of the *Jane Stewart* the valuable nets belonged to four members of the crew, on whom the loss fell; the vessel was privately owned, the crew having no share in her.

Skipper Stewart stated that altogether eleven fishing vessels were destroyed that night by the submarine, and so expeditiously and systematically was the ruthless work done that he calculated that on the average one vessel was destroyed every sixteen minutes.

This onslaught in the night was wanton, cowardly and from the German point of view entirely useless. The enemy hoped by such a display of "frightfulness" to drive the fishermen from the seas and so to fill them with terror that they would not go to sea again; yet such was the unaccountable mentality of the Briton that he not only persisted in setting forth again in his little vessels to catch the fish, but in doing so he often did his best to evade the very measures that were taken to protect him. Something more was needed to cow him than fearsome Teutons, even when they pointed huge revolvers at unprotected and defenceless men, and had the added horror of glistening axes depending from the belts encircling their impressive waists.

# CHAPTER 11

# Keeping the Trade Routes Clear

I am in a mine-sweeper. We just have to sweep the seas every day, keeping the trade routes and passages clear of mines, so that the merchant ships can arrive and leave our ports in safety." So wrote a fisher lad at the end of three years of war, and he summed up part of the most vital work of the sweepers, "keeping the trade routes clear." "It's not a very nice job," he explained. "We are away from home for so long. It's a very rough life." Then the fisherman's philosophy came to his rescue and dispelled the gloom. "But we mustn't grumble, as we have been spared so far, while so many of our mates have been killed; and when we consider what a lot of suffering there is at the present time it makes you forget all about your little discomforts and troubles as long as you are in good health.

That letter was one of many which were written in the same strain by fishermen and fisher lads who had forsaken the drift-nets and the trawls for sweeping and patrol work in the North Sea and any other sea to which they were sent. It was "not a very nice job," and it was "a very rough life," they were all agreed on that point; but there had been nothing nice or easy in the fishing life to which they had been accustomed. In the changed existence, however, there had to be added to the ordinary risks of fishing the vastly increased danger arising out of the war, the ever-present peril of the mine in particular and the submarine and other enemy craft. It was impossible to go to sea in home waters or towards enemy and allies' coasts without incurring constant peril—and many a little vessel carried on her work almost in the jaws of Germany.

Of sweepers and patrollers that were lost in carrying out their du-

THIS CREW OF A NORTH SEA TRAWLER IS SHOWN, WITH
TWO EXCEPTIONS, IN NAVAL UNIFORM BELOW.

THE ABOVE CREW IN NAVAL UNIFORM, AS THE COMPLE-
MENT OF ONE OF HIS MAJESTY'S TRAWLERS.

ties the number was large in the first three years of war. Owing to the method of work—these vessels operated in company—a serious loss, when it took place, was known, and the cause of it, mine, torpedo or gunfire, was ascertainable, but there were numerous instances of craft disappearing and leaving no trace behind them.

Some deep roar in the night would be heard, accompanied by a terrific flame, and it would be known later, because a particular vessel did not return from sea, that doubtless she had met her fate through striking a mine. Or the explosion would be seen and heard in the daytime, and there could be no question as to the time and manner of a little steamboat's fate.

Such casualties were reported in connection with peaceful fishing, as well as warlike operations. Take the case of a Lowestoft smack which had gone trawling. This was long after the war began, when the arrangements concerning fishing made by the naval authorities had reached a state of considerable perfection, and everything which experience could suggest had been done with the two-fold object of protecting the fisherman and enabling him to carry on his work.

The smack carried a crew of five and she was on a fishing-ground. Another smack was about four hundred yards away, and her crew were hauling the gear when they heard a loud explosion and saw a large column of smoke on the water. The skipper at once hauled his gear and went to the wreckage, lowered his boat, and made a search. All that was seen of the crew of five was the skipper, floating in the wreckage. He was picked up and taken on board the rescuing smack, but he had been terribly injured and was dead. All that it was possible to do in this case was for a coroner's jury to say that the skipper met his death through his vessel being blown up by a mine. That was one of the inevitable hazards of the sea in war-time, and a danger which was constantly met by those who kept the trade routes clear.

That wonderful system of sea clearance was in full operation very early in the war, and those who visited the North-East coast at the time of the panic-stricken bombardment by runaway German warships in December, 1914, had an opportunity of seeing the sweepers at work, for they were operating close inshore, in that great North Sea fairway between the Tyne and the Thames, in which the Germans had sown a large number of mines.

In appearance the gallant little steamboats differed only slightly from their aspect when trawling, the chief alteration being that they did not look quite so independent and had more cohesion and orderliness in their movements than when they were scattered over a wide area fleeting or single-boating.

From the cliff-top, gazing seaward into the winter mist which was half a fog, they looked like storm-birds keeping company and replenishing their larders. And they were something of both, for they had the wind and sea to fight, and they were anxious to add to their score of captured or destroyed mines.

A dull crash told of the destruction of a mine—a crash which had the effect of causing a rush to shelter of people in an adjacent undefended port who had lately endured a cowardly bombardment and many of whose homes were in ruins. In the streets were little children, with heads and limbs bandaged, but incorrigibly cheerful, who had been at play when the German guns began to fire and by chance hit something which was not of military importance, though in Germany they had wild official tales of brave attacks on "forts" and "fortresses." These youngsters could tell a good deal about the raid, and they could sell pieces of German shell, large or small, according to the price paid. They understood the sweeping, too, for most of them were children of fishermen, and some of their fathers were out on the grey sea in the little ships with the high bows and low after-part, sharing in the drag which was clearing the lane between the two great rivers.

From that high cliff it was as impressive to watch the sweepers as it was to see the procession of steam and sailing vessels going north and south, as if no such thing as war existed, and certainly as if the German Navy had no being. Already great and good work had been done by the sweepers. The work was a continuation of the task which had been started at the very beginning of the war, and was never to be relaxed while the war continued. How long it was to be maintained when peace returned time alone was to show; but it was known that whenever the fighting ended there would be still a long hard task before the sweepers, and that many a peril would have to be faced by sweeper and fisher before the last of the German devilries had been cleared away.

To watch the steamers and sailing vessels, big and little, going their appointed ways to north and south in comparative security was a powerful reminder of the wonderful work which even at that early stage these sweepers were doing. Inshore were the sweepers, keeping the lane clear; away out upon the waters were patrolling warships, and beyond them it was certain that there were more and bigger ships of war, waiting for the Germans, who, however, had learned wisdom, and did not come.

In peace time this famous North Sea lane was a continuous line of shipping, and it was no uncommon thing to count, from any such point as the cliffs at Whitby or Scarborough, forty or fifty steamboats, large and small, tramps and colliers predominating, for the Loudon liners went southabout; while from Flamborough Head the number was greater still.

So vast was the peace-time traffic on this particular lane that one time, in Bridlington Bay, during a prolonged North-Easterly gale, more than seven hundred vessels had sheltered at the same time. That was a gale, in November, 1893, in which there were many heavy losses in the North Sea, yet it was safely ridden out by great numbers of smacks and steam trawlers which had no chance of running to shelter.

From the Tyne to the Thames that lane extended, and what applied to that locality applied also to the entire coast. There were clearly defined tracks at sea for traffic, and it was because these tracks were so well swept and protected that it was possible for the Admiralty to make the astonishing weekly returns of arrivals and departures of ships. These were numbered by the thousand, even when the unrestricted warfare of the German submarines had reached its zenith.

These lanes were of paramount importance, and in so far as human skill and courage could accomplish the task they were kept clear of mines and submarines. But there was one lane above all others which needed the ceaseless attention of the sweepers, and that was the lane between England and France by which millions of fighting men and non-combatants were conveyed in safety out and home. Imagination—and even that elastic gift might not succeed—could conjure up a picture of the frantic and despairing efforts of the Germans to interfere with and damage or destroy that vital lane; but nothing that the enemy could devise, nothing that he did, nothing that at the summit of his devilry, when he drew no distinction between hospital ship and battleship, he attempted, had the least effect upon the lane. His submarines slunk around, only to be destroyed, captured or kept at an innocuous distance; and as for his mines, sown broadcast, with no thought for friend or neutral, they were gathered in to swell the reapers' harvest or were blown up or sent to the bottom of the sea.

In doing all this work in the Channel, with Dover as the base, many acts were performed by drifters and trawlers of which occasionally the public learned something from official statements, and these fishers had their share in the renown of the Dover Patrol.

The exceptionally severe winter of 1916-'17 added greatly to the privations of the men who were mine-sweeping, patrolling and fishing. So terrible was the cold that German sailors who were killed in the fight with the British during the early morning of January 23 were encased in ice when the battered destroyer V69 entered Ymuiden, and the bodies had to be dug out with axes. An arm that was shot away was found frozen in the rigging. These incidents indicated the severity of the weather in which British fishermen of all sorts on the North Sea were carrying on their varied work.

Heavy losses were sustained, apart from the casualties of war. On January 25, 1917, three British trawlers and a smack were lost, the smack being the *Ethel*, of Ramsgate, and the trawlers the *Lucy*, the *Gladys*, and the *Star of the Sea*. When the crews of the trawlers were landed they stated that they had been in open boats for seventeen hours.

During the whole of that time these fishermen had suffered intensely from exposure, but happily, in their cases, as in all instances like them, help and comfort were at hand as soon as they reached haven. As a rule plenty of clothing, food, fire and rest were available; and when supplies ran short there were always fellow-fishermen ashore who took off their own boots and some of their clothing and lent them to the sufferers who had come in from the bitter sea after prolonged exposure.

Survivors remained ashore only long enough to pull round, then, at the call of duty and the need of making a living, they found fresh ships and went back to sea.

CHAPTER 12

# Drifters and Cruisers:
# a Skipper's V.C.

Three years of war passed before a Victoria Cross was awarded to a fisherman. During that period the awards of 306 Crosses had been gazetted, the vast majority of these having gone to the Army, and a small minority to the Navy. In all the number of Crosses won by the Navy was 15, and of these 5 went to the Royal Naval Reserve, of which the Trawler Section formed a part.

There had been many uncommonly brave deeds by sweepers and patrollers, acts which had been recognised by the bestowal of distinctions; but the hope that the greatest honour of all would fall to one at least of the heroic fishermen was slow of realisation, and it was not until the affair of drifters and cruisers in the Adriatic occurred that a member was chosen as a recipient of the Cross. This was Skipper Joseph Watt, R.N.R., who had joined the naval service on January 11, 1915, and his valour was recorded in the *London Gazette* of August 20, 1917, in the following details:—

For most conspicuous gallantry when the Allied drifter line in the Straits of Otranto was attacked by Austrian light cruisers on the morning of May 15. 1917.

When hailed by an Austrian cruiser at about 100 yards range and ordered to stop and abandon his drifter, the *Gowan Lea*, Skipper Watt ordered full speed ahead and called upon his crew to give three cheers and fight to the finish. The cruiser was then engaged, but after one round had been fired a shot from the enemy disabled the breech of the drifter's gun. The gun's crew, however, stuck to the gun, endeavouring to make it work, being under heavy fire all the time. After the cruiser had passed on, Skipper Watt took the *Gowan Lea* alongside the badly damaged drifter *Floandi* and assisted to remove the dead and wounded.

It was not until the *Gazette* announced the award of the Victoria Cross and other distinctions in connection with this fight between cruisers and drifters that it was possible to get a clear understanding of what had happened in the Straits of Otranto. No explanation had been given as to the origin of the affair; but a few weeks earlier Admiral Viscount Jellicoe, in a public speech, had mentioned the case of a gallant skipper in the Adriatic, who proved to be Watt.

It was stated by the admiral that the drifter's weapon was a six-pounder. He also mentioned the case of one of the hands who had his leg shattered, but continued at his gun and fired it throughout the action. This was the spirit, remarked the Admiral, which would never allow us to be defeated; this was the spirit which would win the war—and he hoped win it quickly. The *Gazette* showed that that gallant hand was Deckhand Frederick Hawley Lamb, R.N.R., Trawler Section, who, "though severely wounded in the leg by the explosion of a box of ammunition on H.M. drifter *Gowan Lea*, stuck to his gun, endeavouring to make it work."

For his courage and devotion to duty Lamb was awarded the Conspicuous Gallantry Medal. He was a married man, with a family of six and lived in Fraserburgh. His leg was broken in two places and he was taken to an Italian hospital.

Skipper Watt also belonged to Fraserburgh, but was a native of Gamrie. He was 30 years of age, married, but without family. He already had been under fire in the little *Gowan Lea*, and had had a narrow escape, in the previous December. On that occasion the skipper was in his cabin when a shell passed right through it. The funnel was blown away and several of the crew were killed. The boat was lowered, with the compass on board, but it was sent to the bottom by a shell.

The enemy ships were driven off; but Watt was now in the singular position, not having a compass, of being unable to locate himself. He saw another patrol vessel, and headed his damaged craft for her, but the other vessel, mistrusting the funnelless *Gowan Lea*, and assuming that she was some unknown foe, made off under full steam.

It spoke well for the power and handling of the *Gowan Lea* that in spite of her crippled state and the heavy handicap of the lost funnel she overtook the other craft, and, of course, got all the help she needed. One can readily picture that strange flight and pursuit and the appearance of the brave little ship which had survived such a severe punishment

Skipper Watt had as companions in Otranto Straits five gallant skippers to each of whom the Distinguished Service Cross was awarded for remaining at his post "under the fire of a very superior force"; and these were but selected cases from many fine examples.

There was Skipper William Bruce, who, with his crew, held on until his drifter, the *Quarry Knowe*, blew up.

The drifter *Taits* was badly damaged and in a sinking state through the enemy's very heavy fire; but Skipper Robert Stephen remained at his post; and the same fine tribute was paid to Skipper William Farquhar, who only left his drifter, the *Admirable*, when she was sinking.

Very gallant was the conduct of Skipper Robert Cowe, of the drifter *Coral Haven*, who did as Skipper Watt had done—he kept his little ship "heading for the enemy" and encouraged his crew "to fight their small gun. Four rounds were fired, and he and his crew only escaped from their ship when she was on fire and in a sinking condition."

The fifth member of this heroic band was Skipper Dennis John Nichols, of the drifter *Floandi*, who "remained at his post in the wheel-house, steering his ship, and although wounded himself, assisted in removing the more severely wounded members of his crew." Later Skipper Nichols went in a small boat, and by plugging the holes which had been made in the drifter's side enabled her to reach port.

The records contained other little stories which, though brief and incomplete, gave an insight into what had been done in the Adriatic against overwhelming odds.

It was amazing that drifters had done so much and cruisers so little, for the odds against the tiny fishing craft were overwhelming. The drifter was a mere toy on the water compared with the bulk of even an enemy light cruiser, and the toy had no protection in the shape of armour, no weapon except one six-pounder gun. That disparity of force must never be forgotten in considering the fight of the drifters and cruisers in the Adriatic.

There was a rousing display of courage and endurance by Engineman Charles Mobbs, R.N.R,, who stuck to his post until the main steam-pipe was shot away. This meant, in the cramped space of a drifter's engine-room, that Mobbs was in a death-trap. He was forced to leave; but his absence was only temporary, and as soon as he could do so he made his way back and put out the fires.

Engineman Mobbs doubtless looked upon that dangerous work as being merely part of his duty; but he did it nobly, and did more, for he went in a small boat and helped to plug holes which had been made in the vessel's side by enemy shots. By doing these things Mobbs helped materially in getting the drifter safely to port.

Let it be borne in mind that the engine-room of a drifter was a small crowded space, that the bursting of the main steam-pipe would fill that space with scalding steam, that there was the constant peril of an explosion from the boiler, and that it was uncommonly hazardous to reach the dark, cramped stoke-hole, an even worse place than the little engine-room; add to these risks the chance of the shattered vessel foundering, or a shot smashing and sinking her, and something approximating the true picture will arise in the mind and show what happened in Otranto Straits.

Courage of the very highest type was shown by Second Hand John Turner, R.N.R., in performing an act the like of which had been recognised on many occasions by the award of the Victoria Cross. Turner saw that the enemy were making determined efforts to destroy the wireless telegraphy apparatus of his little ship, and with the coolness that he would have shewn on the North Sea in climbing he went aloft to strike the topmast, regardless of the fact that shells were passing between the mast and the funnel. This achievement came under the heading of conspicuous gallantry and Turner was awarded the medal.

Uncommon heroism was shown by another second hand, Joseph Hendry, R.N.R. His ship was in a sinking state and the rest of the crew left her in a small boat and were taken prisoners; but Hendry refused to leave. At last his ship sank under him and he was in the water for some hours until he was picked up by another drifter. Hendry was another hero to whom the Conspicuous Gallantry Medal was awarded.

The undaunted spirit of these driftermen in the Adriatic was shown in many ways, and in the most unexpected fashion. That display of courage must have amazed and disheartened the Austrians on one of the rare occasions when they dared to try a passage of arms with British naval forces.

The crew of the drifter to which Engineman Walter Watt belonged were taken prisoners and they were being conveyed to an Austrian cruiser. Watt had no fancy for imprisonment, and on the way to the enemy ship he jumped overboard. He was recaptured, but again he jumped overboard, and this time his pluck was rewarded by his escape;

but he was not rescued until he had been in the water for an hour and a quarter, and then he was picked up by another drifter. This brave engineman also received the medal for conspicuous gallantry.

To eight deckhands and others the Distinguished Service Medal was awarded, and though in their cases no details were published, it was safe to assume that their conduct was in keeping with the splendid behaviour of the men in the particular cases mentioned.

A bar to the Distinguished Service Medal which he had already won was given to Deckhand Edward Ernest Godbold, R.N.R.

Amongst the officers and men mentioned in dispatches were Chief Skipper H. J. Goldspink, who had already won the Distinguished Service Cross; Skipper W. H. Chaney, Skipper F. Hutchings, Skipper G. Thain and Skipper E. E. Snowling; Second Hand A. Gordon, and Trimmer G. Craig, both of whom were killed in action. In addition to these skippers and men there were mentioned Second Hands J. Stephen, A. Smith, A. Findlay, Deckhands J. C. J. Taylor, E. G. Hitter, W. H. Adams, J. Boulton, Enginemen J. Sim, J. E. Cooper, T. Anderson, Trimmer T. Leggat.

No adequate understanding of the complete achievement is possible without bearing in mind the sort of vessel that a drifter was. The *Gowan Lea* was built in 1914 at Fraserburgh, and had a net tonnage of 35 and horse-power of 27. The *Floandi* was built at Yarmouth in 1914, and was of 42 tons and 53 horse-power. The *Quarry Knowe*, 41 tons, 42 horse-power, was built at Aberdeen in 1914; the *Taits* was built at Sandhaven in 1907, and was of 36 tons and 28 horse-power; the *Admirable*, built at Montrose in 19 14, was of 37 tons and 41 horse-power, and the *Coral Haven*, built at Sandhaven in 1913, was of 34 tons and 35 horse-power.

Some of these drifters were of wood and some of steel; but all had made their own way out to the Mediterranean to the mouth of that Adriatic Sea which is called the Straits of Otranto, on one side of which is Italy and on the other side Turkey.

It is worthy of remembrance that these fishing vessels from the grey North Sea went out to another fishing centre in a famous and romantic region which was the scene of Horace Walpole's story, *The Castle of Otranto*, that production which he "wished to be believed ancient, and almost everybody was imposed upon."

So far the official stories of what skippers and other trawler ratings did in Otranto Straits have shown what a stubborn and unequal fight took place, a battle which was in many respects unique in naval annals;

but there were other details which made it possible to get a better understanding of the affair.

It was clear that H.M.S. *Bristol* and *Dartmouth* were engaged and did splendid work. Captain Albert Percy Addison, R.N., received the C.M.G. in recognition of his services in command of the *Dartmouth* "during the pursuit of and running fight with Austrian cruisers which had attacked the Allied drifter line . . . and especially for his excellent judgement and work in bringing his ship safely into port when she had been torpedoed by an enemy submarine on her passage back after the cruiser action was over." Engineer-Commander Frank Rheuben Goodwin, R.N., was appointed to the Companionship of the Distinguished Service Order for exceptional work under very trying conditions in bringing the *Dartmouth* to port after she was torpedoed, and the same honour was conferred upon Captain George James Todd, R.N., for his services in command of the *Bristol* during the action.

These deeds of heroism were not all. The brief official records proved how stern the contest had been and how valiantly the skippers and crews of the drifters had fought their ships. The curt announcement had been made that fourteen drifters had been lost in the Adriatic; then in the casualty lists issued by the Admiralty names of missing men from H.M. drifters were published. One of these lists, issued in the early days of June, contained the names of no fewer than 67 men, mostly deckhands and enginemen, and it was to be assumed that they had given their lives in battle.

In connection with this affair in the Adriatic the Admiralty subsequently announced that on May 15 an Austrian force consisting of light cruisers, which were subsequently reinforced by destroyers, raided the Allied drifter line and succeeded in sinking fourteen British drifters—*Admirable, Avondale, Coral Haven, Craignoon, Felicitas, Girl Grade, Girl Rose, Helenora, Quarry Knowe, Selby, Serene, Taits, Transit, Young Linnet*—from which (according to an Austrian *communiqué*) seventy-two prisoners were taken.

Skipper Watt had the incurable modesty of the true hero, and like so many of the valiant fighters to whom the Victoria Cross had been awarded, he fled when a public reception was prepared for him. Sometime after he had become famous, and when he possessed not only the Cross but also decorations from the French, Serbian and Italian Governments, he had leave of absence and made for his Scottish home—a longed-for change, after his hard experiences and a spell in hospital. News of his return reached Fraserburgh, and, rightly enough, the proud townspeople determined to do him honour. It was arranged that the Town Council and the magistrates, supported by the local volunteers, should attend at the railway station and welcome the hero; but the gallant skipper heard of these unwanted honours and outwitted the promoters as completely as he had got the better of the enemy cruisers. He so arranged things that he reached Fraserburgh by the last train, arriving on a dark November night, and as no one knew of his arrival, he got home unnoticed and unrecognised. Soon after his arrival his wife presented him with a son and heir, and this the V.C. hero declared to be the greatest honour that had been conferred upon him. Skipper Watt received his Victoria Cross from the King at Buckingham Palace on April 6, 1918.

During a visit to England Skipper Woodgate, of the *Koorah*, gave an insight into the sort of work that the trawlers had done in the Dardanelles.

"When we were up in the Dardanelles," he said, "there was what we call three groups—one, two and three—and each group had to go up, one at a time. The vessel I was in belonged to the second group. The night we were going to make the final dash in the Dardanelles, up to the Narrows, we went, no lights up, everything covered in. They let us get right up to the Narrows, and as we turned round to take our sweeps up, one of our number was blown up. Then they peppered us from each side, from one-and-a-half to two miles. We heard cries for help. I said, 'We shall have to do the best we can and go back and pick up.'

"There was no waiting, no saying 'Who shall go?' As soon as I called for volunteers, three jumped in. I kept the vessel as close as I could to shelter them. I did not think any would come back alive, but no one was hit, and I said, 'Now we'll get the boat in.' Just as we got the boat nicely clear of the water, along came a shot and knocked it in splinters.

"I shouted, 'All hands keep under cover as much as you can!' and I got on the bridge and we went fall steam ahead. I could not tell you what it was like, with floating and sunken mines and shots everywhere. We got knocked about, the mast almost gone, rigging gone, and she was riddled right along the starboard side. One of the hands we picked up had his left arm smashed with shrapnel. That was all the injury we got. When we got out, the commander came alongside and said, 'Have you seen any more trawlers?'

"I said 'Yes, we've got the crew of one aboard, the *Manx Hero.*' We were the last out, and I can tell you, I never want to see such a sight again!"

Subsequent to the telling of that tale, which said so little and yet revealed so much of the readiness and heroism of fishermen at the Dardanelles, a special supplement to the *London Gazette* was published on August 16, 1915, from Vice-Admiral J. M. de Robeck. The dispatch, which was dated July 1, described in detail the part which was played by the British Navy in the landings on the Gallipoli Peninsula on April 26, and it contained a list of awards for services rendered by the Navy at the Dardanelles. The dispatch showed that in the first landing, north of Gaba Tepe, which was carried out under the orders of Rear-Admiral C. F. Thursby, C.M.G., the squadron included fifteen trawlers; and fourteen trawlers were included in the squadron which carried out the lauding at the southern extremity of the Gallipoli Peninsula, under the orders of Rear-Admiral R. E. Wemyss, C.M.G., M.V.O.

In the landing of troops, guns and stores under exceptional natural difficulties and an annihilating fire from artillery and machine-guns and rifles, brave work was done by the trawlermen, and the Admiral reported that innumerable deeds of heroism and daring were performed.

The brief references which had been made to the *Floandi* were followed in the course of time by one of those official announcements which so often told the tale of noble heroism. The Rear-Admiral commanding the British naval forces in the Adriatic forwarded to the Admiralty "the wireless telegraph log of H.M. *Floandi* as an exhibit for the National War Museum"; and in doing so he gave the following facts concerning it:—

This log was found in this condition in the wireless operating cabin of H.M. drifter *Floandi* after an attack on the drifter line by three Austrian cruisers in the Adriatic on May 15, 1917. The wireless operator, Douglas Morris Harris, A.B., R.N.V.R., continued to send and receive messages, although the drifter was being riddled by shells, until he was killed by a piece of shrapnel whilst writing in the log. The piece of shell perforated the log, and the line made by his pencil when he was hit and collapsed can be seen on the page upon which he was writing. The operator was found dead in his chair, lying over the log.

This was one more story of cool courage to add to the already long record of brave deeds which stood to the credit of the men in trawlers, drifters and patrol boats on many seas.

Amongst decorations which had been conferred by the Allied Powers on officers and men of the British Naval Forces for distinguished services during the war were silver medals for military valour conferred by the King of Italy. These awards, announced by the British Admiralty on November 17, 1917, included silver medals to Chief Skipper H. J. Goldspink, D.S.C.; Chief Skipper J. Watt, V.C.; Chief Skipper D. J. Nichols, D.S.C.; Chief Skipper D. Watson, Skipper A. C. Bruce and Skipper P. Reid. Awards of bronze medals for military valour conferred by the King of Italy included the following recipients:—Chief Skipper A. Lyall, Skipper F. Newton, Skipper W. Pi. Maunder, Skipper W. Farquhar, D.S.C.; Skipper R. Scott, Skipper R. Stephen, D.S.C. Skipper J. Strachant, Skipper R. Cowe, D.S.C.; Skipper D. S. Ralph, Skipper W. G. Smith, Skipper W. G. Mayhew and Skipper J. Findlay.

A number of trawler ratings of lesser rank were included in the list of awards of the silver and bronze medals, so that in this particular batch of honours conferred upon naval officers and men there were no fewer than eighteen skippers, of whom one was a V.C. man, and five had already won the Distinguished Service Cross. Though no special locality of the service done was mentioned, it was reasonable to assume that the sphere of operations specially concerned Italy.

Some indication of the steady, quiet work of the fishermen who were serving in the Navy was given by a list of honours, decorations and medals published by the Admiralty on April 6, 1918. The announcements related to services between January 1 and December 31, 1917, and amongst the recipients were four chief skippers and seven skippers, to whom the Distinguished Service Cross had been awarded. Forty-eight second hands, engine-men and deckhands—including "2nd Hand R. W. Forsyth (later Sub-Lieut. R. V. R.")—received the Distinguished Service Medal; and four chief skippers, thirteen skippers and forty-four other ratings were mentioned in Dispatches. All these awards were for services in vessels of the Auxiliary Patrol. For services in action with enemy submarines two skippers received the Distinguished Service Cross; one deckhand the Distinguished Service Medal; five skippers were mentioned in Dispatches, and one second hand received the Distinguished Service Medal. All these recipients were members of the Royal Naval Reserve,

CHAPTER 13

# National Tributes

On Monday, October 29, 1917, Parliament, with deep gratitude, acknowledged the devoted services of the Navy and Army during three years of unparalleled warfare. The prime minister had the opportunity, of which he took full advantage, of paying an impressive tribute to the loyalty and courage of every class of fighter on land and sea and in the air and under water, but as Mr. Asquith, who also spoke, declared, the commonplaces of eulogy or sympathy, though expressed with the art of Pericles or Lincoln, would be meagre and inadequate.

First and naturally came the Navy, said Mr. Lloyd George, who affirmed that it had been the anchor of the Allied cause, and that if it had lost its hold the hopes of the Alliance would have been shattered and Prussia would have been the insolent mistress of Europe and through Europe of the world. He showed in a sentence or two what a colossal task had fallen upon the Navy and how marvellously well that task had been fulfilled. He gave the following figures of men and material transported since the beginning of the war to the British Armies and to those of our Allies:—

| | |
|---|---|
| Men | 13,000,000 |
| Horses | 2,000,000 |
| Vehicles | 500,000 |
| Tons of explosives and supplies | 25,000,000 |
| Tons of coal and oil fuel | 51,000,000 |

Of the 13,000,000 men who had crossed and recrossed the sea, only 3,500 had been lost—2,700 through the action of the enemy, and the remainder through the ordinary perils of the sea. This was apart from the prodigious quantity of food and other materials transported, amounting in all lo 130,000,000 tons transported in British ships. Never before in the history of the world had the British Navy been a more potent and a more beneficent influence in the affairs of men.

Speaking at the same time and on the same subject in the House of Lords, Earl Curzon supplemented these details by saying that 30,000 tons of stores and supplies and 7,000 men were being carried daily to France, and 570 ships of one and three-quarter million tons of shipping were continually employed in carrying troops and stores to all the theatres of war. In 1914 the Navy Estimates provided for 145,000 officers and men; the strength of the Navy now was 430,000. The total tonnage in 1914 was 4,000,000 tons; it was now 6,000,000. Over 3,300 vessels were engaged as mine-sweepers and patrols; the number at the beginning of the war was 12. It was impossible to imagine more arduous or more dangerous duties; yet not a single man had asked to be relieved, and if one man was lost scores and scores leaped forward to take his place.

It was shown in these speeches that men had been torpedoed once, twice—even as often as seven times, and in spite of all had gone back at the earliest moment to confront the perils which they seemed to scorn; and that there were transports which had been torpedoed several times over. About 8,000 men had been lost, said Earl Curzon, yet never a man was found who refused to sail. It was a record which brought a lump to the throat and invested with everlasting fame the British mercantile marine.

So far the details were amazing—so suggestive of magnitude as to be almost incomprehensible and incredible. They showed what the Navy really was, they indicated what the Navy had done and was doing in its terrible silence and solidity, and there was pictured to some extent the part which fishermen had played in more than three long years of war.

A round dozen vessels had grown to the enormous fleet of 3,300; yet even then the picture was not complete, the story was not fully told, however briefly. It remained for Mr. Lloyd George to crown the tribute of the Houses of Parliament with some eloquent and generous sentences, in which he showed how deeply he understood and appreciated the work of the fishermen and the sacrifices they had made. Adding to his statements as to what the Navy as a Navy had done and of the part the mercantile marine had played in the war, the premier said he would like to say a word about the fishermen, whose contribution to the war had been a great one.

Sixty *per cent*, of our fishermen were in the Naval Service. Their trawlers were engaged in some of the most perilous tasks that could be entrusted to seamen—mine-sweeping, "a dangerous occupation, often ending in disaster."

The number of mines the fishermen had swept up was incredible. If they had not done this Britain would now have been blockaded by a ring of deadly machines anchored round her shores. But their service had not been confined to this work. These fishing vessels were found patrolling the seas everywhere, protecting ships, not merely around the British Isles—you found them in the Mediterranean. They surely deserved the best thanks that could be accorded for the services they had rendered.

The premier proceeded from the general to the particular, and gave one or two illustrations of the way in which fishermen had faced these new perils. Here was one case given to him by the Admiralty—a story of a trawler attacked by the gunfire of a German submarine. Though armed only with a 3-pounder gun, outranged by her opponent, she refused to haul down her flag; even when the skipper had both legs shot off and most of the crew were killed or injured. "Throw the confidential books overboard and throw me after them," said the skipper. Refusing to leave his trawler when the few survivors took to the boat, he went down with her.

There was another case of an armed trawler escorting a number of fishing vessels attacked by a submarine. Outranged, her main-boom broken, the funnel down, the wheelhouse blown up, the steering-gear disabled, many of the men killed and the ship sinking, they patched her up with canvas; yet she went on fighting—and when at last she sank the fishing fleet was safe in port.

> These are not men trained to war, (added the prime minister), they are fishermen. But this is the spirit that has animated our sailors, whether in the Navy, the mercantile marine, or our fishing fleets. Never have British sailors, whether in the Navy or in the auxiliary services, shown more grit, never have they rendered greater service to their native land or to humanity. For their courage, for their resolution, for the service they have rendered and for the resource they have shown, I invite the House of Commons in this resolution to thank them, officers and men.

In both Houses this memorable vote of thanks to the Navy and

116

Army was adopted with a unity which showed how thoroughly they realised the vastness of the debt which the Empire owed to the men who had shattered the ruthless devices of the German leaders and the desperate efforts of the German hordes.

A few days after Earl Curzon and the prime minister had paid their tributes to the fishermen, the First Lord of the Admiralty, Sir Eric Geddes, speaking with even greater knowledge of what had been done, added words of praise. This was done in the course of a memorable maiden speech on November 1—a speech in which the First Lord, in the House of Commons, made a comprehensive statement on the naval position.

> Before closing this statement of naval activities, (he said), I would wish to mention the work of the mine-sweepers and mine-layers and of their gallant crews, largely recruited from our hardy fishermen. Both these duties may be offensive as well as defensive. Is it not an offensive measure to lay mines at night in the tortuous channels of the enemy minefields, with the possibility of attack from his patrol craft or discovery and bombardment from his land guns? Similarly, is it not an offensive measure for the mine-sweeper to go into the enemy minefields, which are protected, to sweep a passage, as they have done, to enable their comrades of the submarine or light surface craft to follow in the next night?

Before paying that tribute the First Lord had drawn a striking mental picture of the work done in some quarters by the British Navy. During a recent month the mileage steamed by battleships, cruisers and destroyers in home waters amounted to 1,000,000 nautical miles; in addition there was the ceaseless patrol of the Naval Auxiliary Forces, amounting to well over 6,000,000 nautical miles in home waters in the same month.

The First Lord, in the same speech, referred to a raid on a convoy in connection with which the Admiralty had been severely criticised. This reference was interesting not merely on account of the special subject dealt with but also because it showed again how ubiquitous and helpful fishing craft and fishermen were in the war.

On October 16, 1917, the destroyers *Strongbow* and *Mary* Rose, with three small armed vessels, only one of which was fitted with wireless, escorted a convoy of twelve ships bound from Norway to the Shetland Islands. During the night the small vessel which had the wireless dropped back to screen a ship of the convoy which had to stop owing to her cargo having shifted. The convoy was then accompanied by the destroyers, both of which were fitted with wireless, as well as by two other small craft which were not so equipped.

Just as day was breaking on the 17th the *Strongbow* sighted two ships to the southward, which were closing fast. Visibility was about two miles, and the *Strongbow*, having challenged and received an unsatisfactory reply, at once gave orders for action.

The enemy's first shot wrecked her wireless room and did other damage, and though valiantly fought by her captain and his officers and crew she was sunk.

The *Mary Rose* was immediately attacked by the two German vessels and blown up by a shot in her magazine.

The German ships, which were of a very fast cruiser class, then attacked the vessels of the convoy, sinking nine of them.

It was not until the surviving ships reached Lerwick that the affair became known, and the Admiralty did not receive the information until 7 p.m., about eleven hours after the attack began. The destruction of the wireless installations in the fighting ships, and the enforced dropping back of the wireless-equipped small vessel, prevented the Navy from getting news of the affair and so cutting off the raiders on their return journey.

Hopeless though the odds against them were, the naval forces with the convoy did not hesitate to meet the Germans. The *Mary Rose* was blown up almost at once. The *Strongbow* fought until her guns and engines were out of action, and her commanding officer—Lieutenant-Commander Edward Brooke—who was severely wounded, after his ship was helpless, feeling that she might fall into the hands of the enemy, ordered the engineer officers to stand by to flood the ship, so that she might be sunk rather than captured.

After the *Strongbow* became helpless the enemy's ships returned and swept the decks with small guns.

"The armed trawler *Elise*," the First Lord added, "most gallantly came up to the *Strongbow* to assist in rescuing the crew, but was driven off by the enemy, who returned twice and swept the upper deck of the *Strongbow* with gunfire each time."

Imagination must complete the picture for which the First Lord provided such a substantial basis. To deal only with the "armed trawler *Elise*," it needs but little effort to see her bravely going up to the *Strongbow* to help to save the crew,

A trawler was a mere eggshell compared with such vessels as these German cruisers were—she had no protection whatever against gunfire, and in such an affair the description "armed" was pathetically ludicrous. But the skipper and crew of the *Elise* kept up the traditions of the trawler service just as gloriously as the two destroyers maintained the honour of the Navy.

It was not made clear whether the *Elise* was manned by fishermen or regular naval ratings, but she was at any rate a trawler, and as such her courageous deed must be added to the credit of the trawler service in the war.

Full realisation of the peril of the *Elise* and of her fine achievement was not complete without bearing in mind details of German inhumanity which the Admiralty, previous to the First Lord's speech, had made public. "It is regretted," the official announcement stated, "that five Norwegian, one Danish, and three Swedish vessels—all unarmed—were sunk by gunfire without examination or warning of any kind, and regardless of the lives of their crews and passengers. Lengthy comment upon the action of the Germans is unnecessary, but it adds another example to the long list of criminally inhuman deeds of the German Navy."

It was stated that a small British patrol vessel which arrived at the scene of action picked up seamen from the merchant vessels, this work of humanity being gallantly done under the heavy fire of the German ships. Four of the survivors died on the passage to port. All the neutral survivors condemned the cowardly conduct of the Germans and spoke glowingly of the heroic fight of the British destroyers and of the conduct of the British patrol vessel which rescued seamen under fire. No names were given of the gallant souls on board the *Elise* when she performed the act which made the charming name she bore for ever honoured in the list of charming names which had been bestowed upon practical and very work-a-day trawlers.

This affair, regrettable in so many ways, yet outstanding as a glorious tribute to the valour of the officers and men of the British Navy, took place in a region where so many North Sea fishermen had worked and hardened, in time of peace, for the insistent, stern calls which a prolonged and ruthless war was to impose on them. It was an episode' of the vast area in which the real brunt of the sea fighting and the sea guarding fell—for, as Sir Eric Geddes reminded the House of Commons, the area of the North Sea is 140,000 square nautical miles; we had a coast there, subject to attack by raiders of 566 nautical miles in length, from Cape Wrath to Dover; and the area of vision for a light cruiser squadron, with its attendant destroyers at night was well under five square miles—five square miles in 140,000.

The admiration shown for the work of the sweepers was not confined to Great Britain only, nor to the British Empire; it was not expressed only by the king, himself a sailor, who so fully understood what the sweepers' perils and privations were, and by his subjects of every rank and class; it was a universal admiration, and of all the peoples who showed it none were more generously sympathetic than the French and the Italians. And these tributes were all the more significant because they came from heads of great maritime countries, from fighting men and statesmen who had intimate firsthand knowledge of the conditions of the sweepers' lives and deeds.

The high honour of publishing names in Army Orders was conferred upon gallant fishermen by the French and Italian Governments; of such distinctions was the following, made known in a French Army Order almost to the day on the 112th anniversary of the Battle of Trafalgar and the death of Nelson:—

> B. L. Coburn, R.N.R., fireman in the British Navy, severely wounded in the course of an exploration of a minefield by the explosion of a German mine; Richard Manning, 6926, D.A., deck-hand in the British Navy, seriously wounded by an explosion while engaged in mine-sweeping, who gave proof of remarkable qualities of energy in the course of continual operations of the kind.

That was the text of the Army Order. It was brief, but full of the unique qualities of French expression. There was the "exploration" of a minefield—suggestive of a little world of extreme danger and courageously confronting it; and there was the most happy phrase "deckhand in the British Navy"—a term which gave "deckie" his right and honourable position in the vast scheme of sea power. He was not merely Tom, Dick or Harry of this or that of His Majesty's drifters; he was definitely and permanently set down as Richard Manning, deckhand in the British Navy; and Richard Manning was merely one of a host of brave enduring fellows who risked all and so often gave all for their country and their countrymen.

And such countrymen some of these were, too! So selfish, so callous to everything but their own comfort, so regardless of anybody's safety except their own. On the long coast-line stretching from Dover to the farthest northern point of Scotland the people know too well what three years' war had meant, for there had been brutal bombardments, murder-raids by German airships and aeroplanes and inevitable losses through catastrophes in home and foreign waters.

Silent streets of little houses in fishing ports where Death's hand had fallen heavily, bore tragic witness to extensive sorrow; shattered buildings and wrecked homes in peaceful and non-combatant areas gave further proof of German cruelty and cowardice, yet never a German gun was fired, never a German bomb was dropped which did not harden the determination of these grim sweepers and patrollers and fishers to yield nothing to the enemy, but to fight him to a crushing end.

While this work was in the press the Admiralty issued a report of a German raid on our patrol forces in the Straits of Dover. One trawler, the *James Pond,* and seven drifters—the *Jeannie Murray, Clover Bank, W. Elliott, Cosmos, Silver Queen, Veracity* and *Christina Craig;*—which were hunting a submarine which had been sighted in the patrol, were sunk, and sixty men in these eight fishing vessels were killed. The raid took place at about one o'clock on the morning of February 15, 1918, and was of brief duration.

The real nature of the courage and endurance of these crews of trawlers and drifters was made known on March 16, when the *London Gazette* published details of deeds for which decorations and medals had been awarded. These announcements contained the following cases:—

### DISTINGUISHED SERVICE CROSS.

Skpr. H. Bennett, H.M. Trawler *James Pond.*—Displayed the utmost courage and devotion to duty. Skpr. Bennett ably assisted Ch. Skpr. Berry in his efforts to save the vessel after she had been heavily shelled and set on fire. Attempts were made to put out the fire and to get up the ammunition from below, but both efforts failed, and finally the ship was abandoned. The boat was successfully launched in spite of the fact that the falls had been destroyed by the shelling. The crew got away in her, and succeeded in effecting a landing on the French Coast, where they received every attention from the French authorities.

Skpr. S. A. Head, H.M. Drifter *Vera Creina.*—Displayed gallantry and presence of mind in keeping his ship afloat when badly holed by two 4-inch shells, by' plugging the holes with beds and blankets.

Skpr. J. Mair, H.M. Drifter *W. Elliott.*—Displayed great coolness and presence of mind when his ship was sunk with the loss of seven hands and he himself was injured.

Skpr. J. Turrell, H.M. Drifter *Golden Rule.*—When his ship was severely damaged and ten of his crew had been killed and three badly injured, he displayed great courage and energy in giving orders to the remaining three hands although severely injured himself.

Ch. Skpr. A. E. Berry, D.S.C., H.M. Trawler *James Pond.*—Displayed the utmost coolness and devotion to duty, and behaved in a most courageous manner. His vessel was heavily shelled and set on fire. His cabin was pierced by a shell which exploded and wrecked it, wounding Ch. Skpr. Berry in the legs and setting fire to the whole of the wheel-house. He remained cool and collected throughout, immediately giving orders to all hands to lie down until the firing was over. He then made every effort to get the fires out, and although the hose had been blown to pieces, it was replaced under his directions. Both the attempt to put out the fires and to bring up the ammunition failed, and then Ch. Skpr. Berry gave orders to abandon ship. He refused to abandon his vessel, though offered assistance by a French T.B.D., until he was convinced she was doomed. It was found that the falls of the boat had been destroyed, but the boat was successfully man-handled and launched, and the crew got away in her. Chief Skipper Berry being the last to leave.

CONSPICUOUS GALLANTRY MEDAL.

Engnin. J. Ewing, H.M. Drifter *Violet May*, and Engmn. A. Noble, H. M. Drifter *Violet May*.—For conspicuous gallantry and devotion to duty. When their ship had been very severely handled by the enemy and was on lire forward, and all the rest of the crew had been killed with two exceptions, and those so badly wounded that they could render little or no assistance, Engmn. Ewing and Noble cleared the wreckage of the boom from the small boat, got out the boat, put their wounded shipmates into it, and then took to the boat. Finding the ship did not sink, they returned to her, attacked the fire with buckets, and got it out, small arm ammunition in the wheelhouse exploding as they worked.

They then got their injured shipmates on board again and made them comfortable, afterwards burning flares of old clothes soaked in paraffin until picked up and towed in at 7 a.m. The Vice-Admiral, Dover Patrol, reports:—"The conduct of Noble and Ewing was altogether admirable. Their great gallantry and devotion to duty— and, I would add, their simple modesty—entitles them to very special consideration."

2nd Hand G. B. Rivett, H.M. Drifter *Kosmos*.—For conspicuous gallantry and devotion to duty. He displayed great courage and presence of mind when, first, his own ship having sunk, he went overboard after the small boat which was adrift. Later, he put his lifebelt on a severely wounded engineman of another ship. Finally, he assisted in saving the life of Engmn. Wakerley when the latter became unconscious. He was in the water for over two hours.

### DISTINGUISHED SERVICE MEDAL.

Dkhnd. G. M. Barnes, Dkhnd. M. Beaton, 2nd Hand A. Boynton, Dkhnd. J. Brown, Dkhnd. A. Chambers, Ldg. Dkhnd. W. Gullage, Dkhnd. A. G. Holt, Dkhnd. F. J. Plane, Engmn. A. Sandison, Dkhnd. J. E. J. Sharman, Dkhnd. A. Towner, Engmn. J. H. Wakerley.

Mentioned in Dispatches: Skpr. R. Scott.

There was one special feature in the reports of those truly gallant acts and that was the tribute of the Vice-Admiral, Dover Patrol:—

> The conduct of Noble and Ewing was altogether admirable. Their great gallantry and devotion to duty—and, I would add, their simple modesty—entitles them to very special consideration.

"Their simple modesty" was an expression which was understood by workers amongst fishermen. In the old days it needed uncommon patience and tact to get a fisherman who had done great things to talk about them. For one reason he was not accustomed to boast, and for another he was the last man in the world to labour under the impression that there was anything to boast about.

How terrible was the experience through which these brave men went on that memorable February night was shown by the details which were given in the awards—details which, though very brief, suggested such complete pictures of strife and endurance. "His ship was sunk with the loss of seven hands and he himself was injured." "Ten of his crew had been killed and three badly injured." These extracts told in sentences the dreadful but noble story, for it was known that time after time men who had been through similar experiences in trawlers, mine-sweepers and drifters had gone back to sea without delay and had unflinchingly faced afresh the dangers of mine and submarine and all other enemy devices and ships.

## CHAPTER 14

# Another Skipper's V.C.

There could be little doubt as to the sequel to the story of a skipper's bravery which the prime minister had told briefly to the House of Commons, and within a week of his speech the *London Gazette* announced the posthumous grant of the Victoria Cross to Skipper Thomas Crisp, R.N.R., "killed in action." The statement, moving in itself, was made more impressive by the simultaneous announcement of the award of the Distinguished Service Medal to the skipper's son. Second Hand Thomas William Crisp, R.N.R.

Up to that time more than 300 Crosses had been awarded to the Navy and Army during the war. The great majority of these Crosses had been gained by soldiers, for reasons which were obvious, the Navy having been denied the opportunities of glory which the Army had enjoyed in so many different spheres of action.

The Crosses which had been won by members of the Navy, however, represented deeds of uncommon variety and courage and resource, and prominent even amongst these remarkable achievements was the act for which Skipper Watt was awarded the Cross.

Skipper Watt's bravery had been publicly referred to before it was honoured by the award, and the public were again reminded, by that reference, of the obligation under which they rested to the fishermen who had become part of the Navy.

The affair of the drifters in the Adriatic undoubtedly made a strong appeal to the public imagination and enthusiasm, but still greater emotion was aroused when the story of Skipper Crisp's bravery and devotion was made known. When the details of the affair were published it was stated that Crisp was a Lowestoft man, and naturally very great pride was shown by the fishing community in that port, which was and had been so very intimately and prominently associated with the

MINE-SWEEPERS SPLICING A SWEEPING-WIRE

fishing industry.

In the official story which told of Skipper Crisp's valour no locality was indicated, and the only period mentioned was "An August afternoon, at about a quarter to three."

Singularly appropriate to the valiant deeds which were done aboard her before the end came was the name of the little vessel—and that was the *Nelson*. She was a smack, and was on the port tack and the trawl was shot.

The skipper was below, packing fish, and one hand was on deck cleaning fish for the next morning's breakfast. The skipper came on deck, and seeing an object on the horizon he closely, examined it and sent for his glasses. What he saw left no doubt in his mind as to the nature of the object and its purpose, and almost instantly he shouted, "Clear for action! Submarine!"

The rousing words had been scarcely uttered when a shot fell on the *Nelson's* port bow, only about 100 yards away. "The motor man got to his motor, the deck-hand dropped his fish and went to the ammunition-room, the other hands, at the skipper's orders, 'Let go your gear!' let go the warp, put a dan on the end of it; meanwhile the gunlayer held his fire until the skipper said, 'It is no use waiting any longer; we will have to let them have it.'"

Shell after shell was fired at the smack by the submarine, which was away in the distance. About the fourth shell went through the port bow, just below the water line; "Then the skipper shoved her round."

There was no confusion on board, not even when the seventh shell struck the skipper, passed through his side, through the deck, and cut through the side of the ship.

The second hand, the skipper's son, now took charge, with the firing continuing and the *Nelson* sinking owing to the weight of the water that was pouring into her.

At this stage the gunlayer went to the skipper, to see if he could do anything by giving first aid; but it was clear that Crisp was mortally wounded.

"It's all right, boy—do your best," were the skipper's brave words to the gunlayer: then to his son he said, "Send a message off."

The son obeyed and the message was sent—"*Nelson* being attacked by submarine. Skipper killed. Send assistance at once."

All this time the smack was sinking and there were only five rounds of ammunition left.

The skipper was lying on the deck, and going to him, the son heard him say, "Abandon ship. Throw the books overboard."

The son asked the dying father if they could lift him into the boat; but the skipper was too badly wounded to be moved and he answered, "Tom, I'm done. Throw me overboard."

They left him on the deck and took to the small boat, and a quarter of an hour later the *Nelson* went down by the head.

By this time it was nearly dusk. Throughout the night the crew of the boat pulled. Towards morning they were blown out of their course by a freshening wind; but all that day they continued pulling, having hoisted a pair of trousers and a large piece of oilskin fastened to two oars to attract attention.

Once a vessel was seen and once a group of mine-sweepers, but they passed out of sight.

The weather became finer at night, and this was something to the advantage of the weary men who continued toiling at the oars.

During that second night the boat's crew went on pulling until daybreak, and at half-past ten o'clock in the morning they found a buoy and made fast to it. By afternoon they were sighted and rescued.

Such were the official details of the tragic but glorious episode which gave the Cross to the courageous father and the Distinguished Service Medal to his son. The story showed that Crisp just as surely fought against overwhelming odds as did the *Strongbow* and the *Mary Rose* and other British ships throughout the war. There were differences in detail between the official version and the premier's story; but the variance was not material—it was the essentials that mattered, and the broad facts showed that fishermen in war-time had given proof of indomitable endurance.

A smack was infinitely more helpless than a steam trawler, and afforded even less protection to her little crew; and as for her means of defence, they were clearly indicated by the premier's statement that she carried only a 3-pounder gun. The skipper realised the hopelessness of his case, but one thing only stood out clearly and firmly in his mind, and that was to fight his vessel to the very death. He was almost Grenville come to life again—Grenville who, off the Azores, fought his immortal fight, "the one and the fifty-three."

And Sir Richard said again, "We be all good Englishmen. Let us bang these dogs of Seville, these children of the devil; For I never turned my back upon don or devil yet."

Grenville, mortally wounded, refused to yield, and just as the little *Revenge* went down, so the little *Nelson*, shot-torn, foundered. As to the skipper's request of "Throw me overboard," there instinctively comes to mind the earnest wish of Nelson at Trafalgar that his body should not be cast into the sea.

Skipper Watt in the Adriatic had opened the list of fishermen V.C.'s; Skipper Crisp was soon to share the glory with him, though only as a memory, and these two heroes were doubtless but the advance guard of a noble band of sweepers, patrols and drifters who were to join the rigidly limited ranks of recipients of the greatest honour that a soldier or a sailor can gain.

CHAPTER 15

# Difficulties and Remedies

Inevitable and unforeseen difficulties arose in connection with the fish supply of the country as a result of the war, these obstacles relating not only to the vast fishing industry itself but also to the means of distribution and regulation of prices.

Early steps were taken to remedy the drawbacks, and amongst other bodies there came into existence a special committee, the object of which was to take measures for increasing the supply of fish and augmenting the methods of capture. The name of this body was The Fish Food Committee, the chairman of which was Mr. Cecil Harmsworth, M.P., and a prominent member was Mr. Henry G. Maurice, one of the assistant secretaries of the Board of Agriculture and Fisheries.

The work of the Fish Food Committee was in some important respects a continuation of the operations which had been successfully conducted for some years, under the chairmanship of Mr. Harmsworth, with the object of developing the fishing industry by means of small sailing vessels in which motor engines had been installed.

This enterprise had proved very beneficial, particularly on the South-Western shore, and craft which when dependent on sail alone had proved unprofitable became sources of satisfactory income to fishermen when internal combustion engines were installed.

The Fish Food Committee worked on the basis of giving Government aid to enterprising fishermen, and during the war this system was extended very considerably and proved satisfactory and encouraging, simultaneously arrangements were made by which many hard and fast pre-war regulations were amended or cancelled, so that fishermen might have larger and safer areas in which to work. The result of these alterations was that many prohibited areas were available and such stringent regulations as those which had governed the three miles limit were in abeyance.

The naval authorities, who had an almost incredibly heavy burden put upon them, made special efforts to enable fishermen to carry out their ordinary work, and so it happened that while of necessity vast regions which had been previously open to steam trawlers, drifters and long-liners were put out of bounds, there became available many very useful inshore and other fishing areas.

When the Fish Food Committee came into being one of the first problems it had to deal with was the disposal of an immense supply of food in the form of pickled herrings. It was publicly stated that the quantity of this particular fish available was no less than 150,000 tons.

When war broke out the herring season had made a very prosperous start in the Shetland Islands and the North of Scotland, and there it was that the herrings were mostly available. The fish had been caught and brought ashore in the ordinary way, "gipped" by the Scotch fisher girls, packed in brine in barrels and made ready for dispatch to the extensive Continental markets for which this special form of food was prepared; the countries to which they were ordinarily sent being Germany and Russia. German and Russian peasantry in particular relished and esteemed the herring prepared in this fashion, and with bread or potatoes they were in the habit of making a substantial meal from them.

Generally speaking, the pickled herrings were equivalent to the barrelled anchovies whose rawness and brininess appealed to those who favoured strong *hors d'oeuvres*, and that circumstance presented a somewhat serious difficulty, one, indeed, that became almost insoluble. Very complete measures were taken to explain the value of the pickled herring as an article of food, and detailed instructions were issued as to the best method of cooking; but the efforts were not entirely successful, prejudice and culinary troubles making it necessary eventually for great quantities of the herrings to be sent to friendly countries abroad.

While this setback had to be recorded undoubted success attended much of the work of the committee, especially when a number of thoroughly practical men, with a wide knowledge of all the branches of deep sea fishing, were added to that body. It was not merely a question of catching fish, in itself a very serious and complicated one, but it was also a matter of distributing the catches to the best advantage, a task which proved uncommonly difficult in view of the enormous calls which were being continuously made upon the decreased transport facilities of the country. Considerable latitude was allowed to fishermen, so that no serious obstacle should be placed in their way in carrying on their work, and as a consequence energetic measures were adopted by them to get profitable hauls. Many antiquated vessels were pressed into the service and many primitive and simple devices were adopted, especially in relation to inshore fishing from small craft.

Amongst the many systems of fishing employed was that of using a primitive seine from the beach, a method which was essentially one for fine weather and certain parts of the coast, particularly southern districts where there was no proper harbour accommodation. In these localities half-a-dozen men, with a rowing boat and the net, could make from the sands or shingle a considerable number of shoots and hauls before fatigue and hunger called a rest. In some places the men had but little of the appearance of fishermen, for the skilled hands were otherwise employed; yet good results were possible, for though the catches might be small, the demand was great and high prices were obtainable with no cost whatever for transport, the fish being sold either direct from the boat on the beach or carried to the nearest shop or dealer not far away.

The net employed was of the herring-net type, with approximately the same mesh and with small cork-floats at short intervals. It was about 150 yards long and two yards deep, and at each end there was lashed a stout pole to which a long hauling-line was fastened. For the purpose of shooting the net was stowed in the stern-sheets of the boat, with a man in charge; another man rowed a pair of oars and two men had an oar each, so that the boat had four men in her. She was pulled out for a distance of about 300 yards, two men on the beach having one of the hauling-ropes each. When at the distance mentioned the man in the stern-sheets shot the net, the rowers meanwhile pulling in what was approximately a half-circle. When shot the net formed a semicircular wall in the water and effectively enclosed any fish there might be between that net-barrier and the beach itself.

The boat having returned three men jumped into the surf and the man who was left in the little craft pulled himself along by one of the hauling-ropes until he was at the back of the net, where he stood by. The men on the sands then immediately began to haul in the nets. At the start they were separated by a distance of about 200 yards, but as the net was hauled in and became more and more like the cod-end of an ordinary trawl, they got closer together and at last, when the net was almost clear of the water, they were in a little bunch, splashing ankle-deep in the surf and falling eagerly on the catch, which was put in a pad or tub, or the boat itself. As soon as this had been done the boat was pulled out again and precisely the same operation was repeated, the total time occupied being about half-an-hour.

As a rule the catches were not great, the result of a haul at times being no more than a few pounds' weight, and some even of that small total being immature fish; yet this form of fishing appreciably affected the supplies of food in certain localities, especially as the work was carried on during Sundays as well as week-days. The men were peculiar by reason of wearing a broad waist-band of coarse material which served as a protection from the chafing of the hauling-ropes. Their clothing varied, but it was mostly that of the ordinary longshoreman, and a battered bowler would keep company with a pair of badly worn ordinary boots or shoes.

Sometimes a man would have waterproof overalls, but these gave only slight protection, and generally speaking the men were salt-water soaked up to the thighs. This, however, was a minor discomfort, especially in the fine weather, in which alone the particular method of fishing described could be carried on; and in the majority of cases the men were within easy reach of their homes, where a change of kit and rest were available.

The regulations concerning fishing were necessarily stringent, but occasionally, as local circumstances arose, they were somewhat relaxed to meet particular cases; for example, so that the food supply might be increased, the competent naval authority for Ramsgate, Deal and district issued on August 18, 1917, a proclamation relaxing the severe regulations which governed fishing in the roadstead of the Downs. Previously the limit laid down since the war began in which fishing was allowed off Deal and in Pegwell Bay was only half-a-mile from the shore. A much wider area was covered by the new order, which permitted fishing to be carried on by any method from a point known as Deal Bank, which was approximately a mile and a quarter from the shore.

The concession enabled professional fishermen and anglers to get to the deeper waters of the outer Downs, where fish of many kinds abounded in abnormal quantities, and were of unusually fine and large size. The new order was to continue in force until the end of the following January—a period of nearly six months. This concession was interesting and satisfactory, as showing the; wish and readiness of the naval authorities to make every possible allowance with the object of getting valuable supplies from the sea to augment the food resources of the country. Similar concessions were made in other localities as circumstances arose, and the concessions resulted in great benefit to the fishing community.

Prices of fish fluctuated violently and it seemed impossible to regulate them satisfactorily. The great difficulty of taking effective steps to regulate the price of herrings was instanced by an application at East Suffolk Appeal Tribunal in October, 1917, for the extension of the temporary exemption of a Lowestoft fish buyer. Stress was laid on the great importance of the herring fishing and the fact that it was only with much difficulty that an Admiralty concession had been obtained for the fishing to be carried on. The fishing, it was declared, was one of the most important fishings of the year, bringing in hundreds of tons of cheap and economical food.

On that contention the Secretary stated that that morning he had passed a shop in Ipswich where fresh herrings were marked up at 4d. each. He went to another shop and found that the wholesale price, not necessarily to the first man, was 132 for 14s., which worked out at 1.311d. each. The second shop was selling the herrings at 2½d. and 3d. each, the latter price being to customers who required long credit. The Secretary said there could be no wonder that there was a serious waste of fish if they were retailed at 4d. each; and urged that this was rather against the Board's idea of cheap and economical food.

At that time, in another part of the country, herrings just brought in, and sold in the streets without having passed through shops, were offered at five for a shilling, and were good-sized excellent fish at that. In shops within hearing of the boys who cried the herrings in the street eighteenpence a pound was being asked for haddock. In war-time, just as in the time of peace, the most extraordinary variations were noticeable in fish prices, and it was not easy to fix a standard rate.

It was obvious, however, that the prices of fish, like other food, would have to be fixed, and on January 23, 1918, the Food Controller issued an order establishing maximum retail prices for fish. These new prices varied from 6d. a lb. for such fish as pickled herrings (whole fish) to 4s. a lb. for cuts of salmon. Other prices per lb. were:—Brill and turbot, whole 2s. 6d., cuts 3s. 3d., cod, whole, 1s. 3d., cuts 1s. 10d.; haddock, whole is. 3d., cuts 1s. 10d.; halibut, whole 2s. 6d., cuts 3s. 3d.; plaice, whole 1s. 10d.; soles and slips, whole 3s. 6d.

Under the order very high prices were chargeable for various sorts of fish, which in pre-war days were ranked as "offal." It was soon clear that the Fish (Prices) Order had not made much difference to the value of the catches, for catches from the home ground often realised more than £2,000 each, while a deep sea catch fetched far more. In the Easter period of 1918 trawlers landing at Grimsby had earned up to £8,000 for a single voyage—on one day catches of £7,000 and £8,000 each were recorded. In the same period a Fleetwood trawler, after a little more than a fortnight's absence deep-sea fishing, brought in a catch which realised £8,000, a record for the port.

Strange tales were told of the earnings of skippers and other fishers during the war, tales of fortunes made in a few mouths and of skippers retiring to country mansions on their earnings. Doubtless some of the tales lost nothing in the telling; but there was little doubt that the men employed in ordinary fishing did at times make exceptional incomes, and certainly the industry lost none of its well-known hazard.

If a man had a share in the catches and was not merely a paid hand, with limited wages, then he might and often did receive large sums of money as his part of the vessel's proceeds.

Remarkable figures were given relating to the earnings of Hull skippers, who were paid a percentage of the value of their catches, this averaging £10 on the £100, though some skippers, having a different arrangement, received even more than that proportion. One well-known Hull skipper was known to have earned more than £25,000 during the first three years of the war, another £15,000 in two years; while the balance-sheet of a local firm of trawler owners credited one of the skippers with £8,000 during the year which the accounts covered. All the skippers had shared in the luck of the fishing, and they did not hesitate to say that they had earned all they had got, in view of the perils of fishing in war-time.

At the time these statements were made it was reported that men engaged in the Loch Fyne fishing, where prices had risen to unprecedented rates, had cleared £3,000 in considerably less than a year; and some of the younger men who had only a share in a boat were known to have made £750 in the same period.

Many of the motor fishing-boats did uncommonly well. Two of these vessels which landed their catches at Mallaig made £750 and £700 respectively for a shot of herrings. These sums represented double the price which was asked at the time for an ordinary first-rate motor boat, while a large motor fishing-boat was obtainable for

£550.

When the statements of these extraordinary earnings were first made there was a natural tendency to discredit them, and to believe that they were greatly exaggerated; but the authenticity of the figures was set at rest by the report of the Acting Chief Fishery Officer (Mr. John H. Leng) of the North-Eastern Sea Fisheries Committee for the quarter which ended on September 30. The boats that were left and were working in that district, he said, had all done very well. This was shown by the increased value of the landings over the corresponding quarter of the previous year.

After confirming the figures of skippers' earnings which have been mentioned, Mr. Leng gave statistics which made it clear that such large earnings were easily possible. The total value of all kinds of fish landed had increased enormously, and there would be a further increase in value in 1917, despite the decreased landings. When it was remembered that our fishing fleet had been reduced to 30 *per cent*, of its size before the war, it would be realised that the earnings of the remaining vessels were very large indeed. Some large catches of herring had been landed.

At Hartlepool herrings had realised as much as £14 cran, and at Scarborough £15 was paid, but at that port this price did not continue. Several of the drifters at Hartlepool and Scarborough earned £350 for one night's fishing, and as much as £1,500 for a week's fishing. Throughout the district the men had done very well, especially the motor boat men, who had earned large sums; and the danger seemed to be that in a good many cases, with fish fetching such fabulous prices, the men seemed to stick at nothing.

In a discussion which followed the reading of the report Captain Johnson said he thought that 90 *per cent*, of the money earned by the skippers should be taken from them and given to the men who were fighting for the country; they had no right to the whole of the money. What about the mine-sweepers, who made the sea clear for the fishers? Alderman Moss said that the men who had earned this big money had been fishing off Iceland and the Faroes and had got safely through. Other men had lost life or limb, and their earnings were not stated. There were two sides to the question. Some men had laid down their lives in bringing in food for the people. Captain Johnson then remarked that many others were running the same risk in connection with the commerce of the country, and were getting nothing from it; and another member observed that he had no doubt that the Inland

Revenue would get hold of the successful men.

What the Inland Revenue authorities did in these matters was not known; but the law generally had few terrors for many of the fishermen who were left to carry on the fishing industry. There was a good deal of illegal trawling, the spoils of this exciting operation being so great that in not a few cases skippers persisted in taking the risk of discovery and all the penalties it entailed, knowing that if punishment ended with a fine it could be borne with equanimity.

Well into the fourth year of war two trawler skippers, at Cupar, Firth of Forth, were each fined £80, with the option of six weeks' imprisonment, for fishing in a prohibited area on the East coast of Scotland, and at the same time seven other trawler skippers, for the same offence, were each fined £50, with the alternative of one month's imprisonment, the total amount of the penalties being £510. The sum was large, but what it really meant was shown by the statement in court that these skippers had earned £300 daily by these operations.

Shortly after these remarkable figures were publicly given, a trawler's catch, which was landed at a North-Eastern port, made £5,500. On the basis which has been indicated it is not difficult to estimate the skipper's share. On the very day when the catch was sold cod was fetching 2/- a pound in shops at a seaside town; 1/8 a pound had to be paid for haddock, fresh or dried, and 3d. each had to be paid for very small herrings—fish that were no larger than the Spanish sardine.

In the same town Newfoundland dried salt cod was to be had for 8d. a pound; but to the great majority of housewives this article was as little acceptable as pickled herrings. While these prices were being paid on the South coast, 6d. was asked for a fresh herring in London, even in Farringdon Street; but cut cod was to be had for 1/8 and haddock for 1/- a pound, the great difference in price being caused doubtless by the increased cost of carriage to the South coast, most of the fish going long distances by rail. Local fishing was precarious—for one morning's fishing by a fleet of a score small sailing vessels, each manned by two hands, only a bushel of sprats was secured.

Comparison between these prices and those for the opening of the Grimsby herring season of 1898 may be made. That season began in August with "a rush and a great fall in prices." Owing to the large supply, prices for fresh only ranged from 2s. down to 1s. a hundred, though the fish were of good quality and nice marketable size." "Bloater stuff" made an average of 1s. per hundred.

The huge earnings referred to aroused much comment and caused comparison between the money made by fishermen engaged in the ordinary way and the wages that were paid to fishermen who were sweeping or patrolling; but it was not from the men who were doing the more dangerous work that the criticisms mostly came. They continued their labours quietly and loyally, hoping that when the war was over they too might have the chance to reap a share of the wonderful harvest.

As to the sums which were paid for catches, it was pointed out that merchants bid against each other in the most astonishing manner, and that while certain kinds of fish might be started at the nominal sum of £4 for a particular class of package the bidding would possibly rise to £10. It was urged that the whole evil of the consumer being forced to pay abnormal prices was due to the absence of adequate control of prices at the fountain-head.

While phenomenal incomes were made by a large body of men who were engaged in the deep sea and inshore fisheries, proportionate wages were paid to subsidiary workers ashore—in a law case, for example, it was stated that a lad of seventeen was getting £1 a day as a fish porter at Billingsgate Market.

As the war progressed it became necessary to take steps to regulate wages and pay, and amongst other things the Admiralty appointed a Fisheries Committee for Grimsby to regulate and control the fisheries of that port, with the object of maintaining a regular supply of deep sea fish. A number of prominent trawler owners composed the committee, to which a full naval status was given. The task before this body was not an easy one, and trouble soon arose owing to a new agreement by which crews were called upon to agree to special requirements of the Admiralty. So serious became the situation that a great strike was imminent; but this was averted by holding over certain requirements and making concessions to trawlers' crews which added about £1 weekly to the average earnings of the men.

By the new agreement referred to, trawlers were classed as Navy ships and the crews as men under naval discipline; the result of which would have been that they were not able to leave at will, and, if of military-age, were liable for military service if they joined their ships. The agreement required the men to sign on for the duration of the war and not merely for the voyage. The engineers as a body refused to accept these conditions without further consideration by their Unions, and subsequently they declined to agree to them. With the object of preventing a strike, which would dislocate food supplies, the owners withdrew the agreement until conferences could be arranged and the new proposals considered from local and national standpoints. An application for higher wages was then made by the engineers, and after a good deal of discussion the owners gave an all-round advance with the object of raising the wages to the rate paid on certain trawlers owned locally. This increase represented £2 11s. 6d. weekly wages for a chief engineer, 10s. per trip risk money, £3 5s. 0d. quarter money, paid to all men serving in one ship for three months, and 7s. 6d. per £100 on the ship's gross earnings. The sum of £1 had been given as risk money in most of the trawlers, but no extra percentage on earnings.

The rates of pay of ratings belonging to the Trawler Section of the Royal Naval Reserve were as follows:

| | | |
|---|---|---|
| Second Hands | 6s. per day | Plus war retainer at £1 a month. |
| Enginemen | | |
| Leading deck hand and leading trimmer | 4s. per day | |
| Deck hands | 3s. 6d. per day | |
| Trimmers and trimmer cooks | | |
| Boys | 1s. per day | No war retainer. |

All ratings received a provision allowance of 1s. 5d, per day and a free kit on entry. All ratings (other than boys) received a gratuity of thirty days' pay on discharge, if they had completed twelve months' service unbroken by desertion. The families of these men were entitled to separation allowance. In regard to the crews of hired drifters, these men were formerly employed on a civilian basis, but arrangements were subsequently made to engage them under a special form of agreement by which they would be subject to naval discipline. The standard rates of pay, which were variable to a small extent under local conditions, were as follows:

| | | Orkneys and Shetlands only |
|---|---|---|
| Mate | 6s. 1d. per day. | 7s. 3d. per day. |
| Engineer | 7s. 4d. „ | 8s. 6d. „ |
| Remainder of crew | 4s. 10d. . „ | 6s. „ |

A daily allowance of 1s. 5d. for food was also paid, and the crews received periodical gratuities when they were required to wear uniform. The families were not entitled to separation allowance. Issue of Navy separation allowance to a wife was conditional, primarily, upon the husband being a Naval rating, Marine or Reservist, borne on the books of one of His Majesty's ships, and in receipt of naval rates of pay. It was also necessary that he should allot, voluntarily, not less than 5s. a week in favour of his wife. These rates of pay were in operation for a considerable period, but owing to the greatly increased and growing cost of living due to the war a promise was made in Parliament that the rates should be revised, with the object of making it easier for the recipients to exist on their allowances.

## CHAPTER 16

# Help For the Fishermen

The public were quick to realise their deep indebtedness to the fishermen who, with unflinching fortitude, pursued their work of various sorts at sea, and there was a widespread and generous effort to do something which should help the gallant men to bear their heavy burden.

This benevolence took two forms, directly and actively doing personal work amongst or for the fishermen, or supporting the societies which specially concerned themselves in the welfare of the men and their families.

There were a number of bodies which were more or less associated with the fishermen, but there was one in particular which worked solely amongst them, and this was the Royal National Mission to Deep Sea Fishermen. That well-known organization, when the war broke out, had been doing a rare and uplifting work on land and sea for more than thirty years.

Originally started as a branch of the Thames Church Mission, the Royal National Mission to Deep Sea Fishermen began operations amongst the deep sea trawlers in the days when men and boys spent their lives on the dangerous fishing banks, far from home, with little or nothing to relieve the oppressive monotony of their existence and the sufferings which were inseparable from their calling. If a man fell ill or sustained a serious injury there was nothing for it but to make the best of the matter at sea or send the sufferer home by the carrier or a returning smack.

Occasionally a smack, having a sick or injured man in her crew, would run home with him, but that proceeding was sternly discouraged and the skipper risked discharge as the reward of his humanity. He had been sent to sea to fish, and so make money for his employer, and not to waste the time of the vessel and the crew. That brutal, sordid view was expressed more than once by callous owners, even though they had been themselves fishermen; and that fact of their previous employment indicated how forlorn and almost hopeless was the position of the deep sea fisherman.

There were no means at sea of bettering the lot of the men; they were a race apart, a class to themselves, and they were left to work out their own salvation. Their kindness to each other was limited by the opportunities afforded by breaks in their work, and these, few at any time, were almost non-existent when a small number in a crew had been reduced by even one, for the extra work of the incapacitated man fell upon them and attention to him became an extra burden.

The common ills of life, which could be so easily relieved and dealt with ashore, were grievous at sea, in the wretched hole of a cabin which was the toiler's only place of refuge. The simplest of remedies were taken to sea, if taken at all, and the crudest of methods were employed in seeking cures. Asked if they had any medicines in the fleets—and the question was put so late as in the eighties—a skipper replied that in his own fleet there were some drugs in the smacks; but when the bottles were emptied they were never filled again. "And," he added, "we didn't know what to do with them."

That remark represented the position of the great body of the fishermen. Of recognized remedies they were ignorant and consequently they set to work to concoct medicines which only the iron constitution of a deep sea toiler could withstand—a favourite mixture included a proportion of Stockholm tar and a dash of turpentine, and this the patient swallowed in perfect faith. Pills of fearsome components were made and taken in equal confidence; in fact, the medical and surgical devices were such as one had been accustomed to read of in connection with stoics like the Red Indians or primitive races such as the aborigines of Australia or the blacks of Central Africa.

Such were the conditions on the fishing banks well within the recollection of the middle-aged; such the almost unrelieved sufferings of a race whose corresponding fellows ashore had at their command the finest hospitals and the highest medical and surgical skill.

The advent of the Deep Sea Mission, as the society was fondly called, changed all that dark horizon and brought upon the grey and stormy seas just such help as that which could be got ashore. One of the most famous of the young surgeons of the day went out to the North Sea in the Mission smacks and was amongst the pioneers who swept the deadly *coper* from the banks, brought new life and hope to the toilers, and did much to develop the men who came forward in their thousands in the hour of their country's sternest needs. That young surgeon was Frederick Treves, the man on whose skill and judgement, in later years, a monarch's life depended.

Many a life and many a limb were saved by this pioneer band of doctors, and to their help and guidance was due much of that simple skill with which Mission skippers handled the contents of their well-equipped dispensaries. These Mission skippers were themselves old fishermen and therefore knew exactly what to do and how to do it in cases of emergency. To them indeed it was a wonderful change that was brought about in the floating towns in which most of their lives had been spent.

There was no longer the hopeless outlook on life, the resignation to unmitigated toil and monotony, for there had come into the midst of their fleets the little bethels which for so many of them stood in the relation of the place of worship at home and gave them, side by side with the Gospel, the material and mental recreation which made of so many of them a new race of men. The band of pioneer doctors and Missioners grew, and to become very prominent amongst them was Dr. Wilfred T. Grenfell, who, after spending a long enough time in the fishing fleets to qualify him to do so, took his master's ticket, and soon afterwards went out to the lonely Labrador to take charge of the vast desolate spaces in which the Deep Sea Mission worked amongst a suffering race of fisherfolk and other toilers.

The council of the Mission realised at an early stage of the war that it would be impossible to continue their work in the fleets at sea on the old basis, and accordingly steps were taken by the chairman, Sir William F. A. Archibald, to place the three fine hospital steamers at the disposal of the Government. With this object the chairman wrote to the prime minister and in due course the matter was dealt with by the Admiralty, the result being an intimation that for the time being there was not a suitable opening for the employment of the vessels.

In these circumstances the council continued to make the best use of the steamers, but the day was not distant when the Admiralty, recognising the urgent need of making use of the best steam fishing vessels available, requisitioned two of the Mission Hospital Steamers, the third having been in the meantime taken over in the most generous manner by Sir Charles F. Chadwyck-Healey, as a Hospital Steamer. In this capacity the fine ship, structurally altered to fit her for her new work, did much valuable service in conveying wounded troops and acting as a floating hospital for sailors. The other two steamboats took a noble part in sweeping and patrolling. In each of these cases the Mission crews and skippers were retained, in one case with commissioned rank and in other instances with warrant rank and lesser ratings.

Amongst the Mission officials to volunteer for service at an early stage in the war was Dr. Frederick W. Willway, one of the Medical Superintendents. Dr. Willway was accepted as a surgeon in the Royal Naval Volunteer Reserve, and it was his great satisfaction to remain with the Mission steamer in which he had so often worked afloat amongst the Deep Sea Fishermen. At a later period Dr. Grenfell temporarily left the great work of the Mission, of which he had charge in Labrador, and spent three months on the Western Front as an army surgeon, with the Harvard Medical Unit—an advance guard of the splendid American Army which was subsequently to take its place and stand side by side with the British and French forces in the most vital region of the war.

When forced by circumstances to abandon for the time being the work afloat, the council concentrated on the shore efforts, which had a great scope, for the society had a round dozen institutes on land—Lerwick, the capital of the Shetlands; Aberdeen, North Shields, Hull, Grimsby, Gorleston, Folkestone, Brixham, Newlyn, Padstow, Milford Haven and Fleetwood. Some time before the war broke out operations had begun at Fleetwood, to which port a considerable number of trawlers had been attracted by the good prospects of the Irish Sea fisheries. The branch was progressing satisfactorily, but the developments of the war necessitated a temporary lessening of the Fleetwood efforts, the falling off in this respect being equalised by increased enterprise in other directions.

No effort was spared to help the fighting forces of all classes, the result being that several of the Mission branches became favourite resorts of large numbers of sailors and soldiers. To mine-sweepers and fishermen who were far from home the institutes became particularly welcome as temporary homes, where beds and food could be obtained, and letters written to and received from home. This letter-writing became a most important feature of the work, and proved as great a pleasure to the man as it was a comfort to the womenfolk and children from whom he was separated by many hundreds of miles for long periods. Part of the institute work consisted of attending to sick men, and often enough mine-sweepers and fishermen who had survived disaster at sea through mine, submarine and storm were received at a Mission institute and provided with sorely needed dry, warm clothing and boots, and with hot food, tea, coffee and cocoa.

Many grateful letters of thanks were received by the society from shipwrecked men who had been cared for at an institute; and frequently these thanks were supplemented by letters from naval officers warmly praising the society's work—indeed, one of the most gratifying features of this particular part of the Mission's enterprise was the warmth of the expressions of approval from naval officers of high rank; and the spontaneity of some of these thanks added greatly to their value. In recognition of her services as honorary secretary and treasurer of the Milford Haven and South Wales Mine-sweepers' Comforts Supply Association, Miss Elizabeth Cooper, a member of the council and Honorary Lady Superintendent of the society's institute at Milford Haven, was appointed an Officer of the Order of the British Empire.

The extensive coast-line covered by the Mission's operations made it possible for a fisherman, whatever his special work might be, to keep in touch with the society, and so it happened that if his last place of call chanced to be Lerwick, in the Shetlands, and his next Newlyn, at the Land's End, he could find a home; and to that home he went as surely as the magnet draws the metal. He had absolute faith in the institute, and as often as not put himself unreservedly into the hands of the Lady Superintendent or other head of the branch, this head, in some cases, being one who had been a fisherman himself, and therefore understood precisely what to do.

The perfect and child-like confidence of fishermen who had to deal with the Mission in war-time was well illustrated in a case relating to one of the East Coast institutes. The Lady Superintendent received by post an envelope containing notes of the value of £20. No letter accompanied it, and there was no clue whatever to the sender; but the recipient had little doubt as to the identity of the sender, and accordingly she put the money to the credit of a fisherman who when at that particular port frequented the institute, and who had a bank balance of importance. This action proved to be correct, and when the fisherman again turned up he had the satisfaction of knowing that his money was safe.

Every penny might well have been squandered, for the port was notoriously dangerous to fishermen and mine-sweepers, so much so that parts of it were put out of bounds by the naval authorities. This fisherman, a bachelor, was like many of his fellows, earning large wages, but unhappily he squandered a considerable part of his money in heavy drinking. He never, however, lost touch with the Mission; he always returned to the fold, and was always welcomed. It was undoubtedly helpful to him to get back to the institute and its friendly atmosphere, and he always had the comfort of knowing that his money was secure and available for his use.

The work which the Mission was able to carry on both at sea and on land after the war broke out was invaluable; but there was no part of the undertaking which was of more real worth and aroused deeper sympathy than the consistent labour in connection with the fishermen who were prisoners of war in Germany.

In a previous chapter first-hand details have been given of the cruel conditions which governed the existence of these unfortunate captives, and those conditions would have been infinitely worse and harder to bear but for the ameliorating influence of the Mission and the generosity of the people who helped the special fund which was raised to succour the prisoners.

It was well indeed for the fishermen prisoners of war that there were available the well tried resources of the Mission. Other and splendid organisations there were which did much to relieve the hardships of prisoners of war in general, but the Mission was particularly well equipped to take special charge of the fishermen of all descriptions who had fallen into the hands of a merciless enemy.

Fishermen had been accustomed to very generous living—that was one of the compensations of their hard lot afloat. The fare might be rough, but it was good and liberal, with an abundance of excellent fresh fish as a regular article of diet. Even when the trips were short, as in the case of the long-liners working from Scarborough—a trip usually covering the period between late on Monday to early on Saturday—the men, who rationed themselves, took to sea well filled "grub-boxes," this being largely the work of their devoted women folk. These "grub-boxes" were practically the same in size and shape as the familiar lawyer's deed-box, and the long-liner and his wife or sweetheart had made an art of furnishing it with a wonderful assortment of what the Americans would doubtless describe as "fixings."

In addition to being well fed, the fisherman, as a rule, was thoroughly well clad, and he had need to be that to withstand the onslaughts of prolonged bitter weather on the North Sea. For his fleeting or single-boating work the fisherman had an ample supply of boots and clothing, a very adequate kit; yet it happened in many cases that he lost the whole of these personal belongings when he lost his liberty and that he was not able to get compensation. In some cases he went into captivity a ruined man, and, in the rare event of being given his liberty because he was considered to be past the power of hurting Germany, he had to make a fresh start in life on returning home.

The fishermen prisoners of war were almost without exception in Germany, a few of them being captives in Austria. This proportion was inevitable, for it was mostly the Germans with whom the fishermen came into contact. Rigorous and cruel treatment of fishermen prisoners of war was common at the very outset of hostilities, and these cruelties were practised in defiance of all protests and in opposition to all the laws of civilised warfare; little or no difference being made between peaceful fishermen and recognized combatants. Everything in the internm.ent camps was subordinated to the law of might, and in the winter months the sufferings of the captives were intense.

At the earliest opportunity steps were taken by the Mission to alleviate these hardships. The ordinary resources of the society were utilised, then, as the demands grew greater, special appeals were made to the benevolence and generosity of the public, and these appeals, never made in vain by the Mission, met with a prompt and liberal response which showed how warm-hearted was the appreciation by the public of the efforts of the fishermen in their country's cause.

Substantial financial help was forthcoming, the administration being mostly left to the society though in certain cases subscribers took upon themselves the maintenance of one or more prisoners of war, week by week, up to the point covered by five shillings a head. This sum, though not great in itself, was yet sufficient to augment considerably the inadequate provision made by the Germans for their prisoners of war; it provided just those comforts which were essential to the health of the captives, while as for their happiness, it was possible to do much with supplementary gifts of tobacco and boots and clothing.

Sympathetic letters, too, were written, and correspondence maintained between the prisoners and their homes. So it happened that in the homes wives and families knew how their husbands, fathers and sweethearts fared, and in the prison camps those who were in bondage heard of what was happening at home.

There were prisoners who became fathers, yet knew nothing of their children except what a photograph showed or a letter told; and there were babes who grew up and first lisped of the "daddy" they had never seen, then talked of him as growing boys and girls.

The weeks, the months, the years passed for these men, and their sorrowful lot became supportable only because of the hope within them, never crushed, that all would be well in the end. Some line-spirited letters and cards were sent from Ruhleben and other camps, indicating the unconquerable spirit of the deep sea toiler.

At the close of 1916 steps were taken officially to make the best use of all existing organisations in connection with beneficent war work, one great object being the prevention of over-lapping and wastage of energy and material. So far as the fishermen prisoners of war were concerned, the Mission was selected by the Government as the channel through which help for the captives should go, and steps were immediately taken to extend the work at the Fishermen's Institute at Grimsby.

At this important branch, guided by the Lady Superintendent (Miss Newnham), a very busy work had been unceasingly carried on, and there was now an unbroken despatch of parcels to the captives, while from the Mission's headquarters at Gorleston there were sent those supplies of tobacco without which life was almost insupportable for fishermen.

In every way the Mission took the best available steps to relieve the hardships of the fishermen prisoners and to make their unhappy lot more endurable. The success of these efforts was evidenced by letters received from the prison camps, and captives frequently declared that without these parcels of food, boots and clothing life in the German prison camps, especially in winter, could not have been supported.

While the society's work was kept steadily going at so many points ashore, it became possible, with the hearty co-operation of the naval authorities, to detail a Mission smack for service amongst the fishermen who were attached to the Grand Fleet. This enterprise was so successful that subsequently another Mission smack was sent to the Grand Fleet, the two vessels serving the purpose which they had for many years carried out amongst the toilers of the deep.

At one period the Mission was in the happy position of finding no fewer than three of its vessels attached to the Grand Fleet—the two smacks referred to and one of the hospital steamers. Simultaneously, with the object of helping the food supply of the country, another Mission smack was specially equipped and sent trawling, and this work she carried on with marked success.

A list of fishermen who were detained as prisoners of war in Germany was issued by the Board of Trade in the early autumn of 1917. Of these prisoners 138 belonged to Grimsby, 65 to Boston, 26 to North and South Shields, and 18 to Hull. There were 222 interred at Ruhleben, 81 at Brandenburg, 13 at Dulmen, 10 at Hamelm, 2 each at Ströhen and Soltau, one each at Karlsruhe and Haveburg, and 10 at places unknown—making a total of 342.

Three fishermen had died in captivity and 21 had been released. The crews or individuals belonged to 57 vessels owned at Grimsby, Hull, Boston, North Shields, Aberdeen, Fleetwood, Montrose, Aberystwyth, Deal, Hartlepool, West Hartlepool, Granton and Whitby.

These fishermen prisoners of war made the best of their captivity. The restrictions imposed upon them with regard to correspondence were severe, and often enough only postcards were sent through by the men to their families or friends.

A large number of people in England interested themselves in the captives, and ladies, in particular, acted as intermediaries between the men and their families, and maintained a correspondence which might not otherwise have been in existence, because the men themselves in some cases had little aptitude for writing, and their wives had less.

These lady correspondents were able to keep in close touch with the women folk and children and tell them, either verbally or by letter, how the prisoners in Germany were faring. If a man in an internment camp sent news of general interest, this would be made known by one or more of the lady correspondents, and so an anxious wife or mother at home would have news of a husband or son which would not have been otherwise obtainable.

One skipper who was interned at Brandenburg wrote, in October, 1917, to one of these correspondents, saying how glad he was to hear that his children had safely received a postcard he had sent. He was longing to hear from them and from his wife again. His correspondent was taking a holiday, and the skipper wrote:—

> I know I shall think myself very lucky when I am able to take my wife and children for their holidays again. You say that the flowers which grow outside your window are small but cheerful and remind you of my ship. Well, that (meaning his trawler) was just the same to me—small but cheerful and homely.

This skipper sent several picture postcards, of which he was allowed to forward only a limited number, and in one of which he was shown with an Englishman on his left and a Frenchman and a Russian seated with him, while standing behind was a Belgian officer. Another photograph showed prisoners of war at this camp amusing themselves by sailing little toy yachts, a recreation which seemed very much like the scenes associated with the Serpentine and other waters in London parks.

In many ways the prisoners did their best to pass the weary time pleasantly and profitably, though it was not easy to do either, one of their forms of recreation being the making of models. Amongst these were some remarkably good scale models of motor launches and other craft. These articles involved the expenditure of a vast amount of time and patience, but those were cheap commodities, and so perfect was the workmanship in many cases that the finished article was worthy of association with the wonderfully perfect and detailed models which were produced by French sailors who were prisoners in England during the Napoleonic wars.

CHAPTER 17

# The Fourth Year

It was impressive and astonishing, at the beginning of the fourth year of war, to visit fishing-ports and see how tenaciously the fishermen pursued their calling and how well supplied they kept the market; one felt for them almost the admiration which was aroused at the sight of the mine-sweepers and patrollers, who gave cause for pride and admiration indeed, for their courage and resource were as wonder compelling as their methods. At Grimsby, for example, the world's largest fishing-port, at the amazing fish-dock, which is the development of the old pontoon—Grimsby is proud of the fact that no other fish-dock is called the pontoon—there was an energy and vigour shown in handling the landed fish which would have struck gloom to the depths of the German heart.

There were long rich rows of "live" cod—the "live" is the complete fish, as opposed to the gutted carcase, and is therefore perfectly fresh and commands the highest market price—and vast *vistas* of boxed haddock and kindred "offal," though in war-time "offal" fetched "prime" prices. The total catch could not be compared with the huge catch of peace time; but it was a strong tribute to the men who had ventured out to sea to get it, and reflected glory on that mighty Navy whose protection had made the fishing possible, for the fish, without exception, had been caught in dangerous waters; yet, hidden mine and submarine notwithstanding, it had been brought to market and the precious food had been put ashore to be distributed throughout the country.

Men were buying and selling and handling the catches just as if no such thing as war existed; the trawlerman was getting ready to leave his vessel for his snatch of change and rest ashore, the sweeper and patroller were doing the same, and when they were not so employed

EXPLODING A MINE WITH RIFLE-SHOTS

they were finishing their preparations for again putting to sea.

Away from the pontoon men were hurrying home, meeting other men, with their kit-bags slung over their shoulders, making for their ships. The home-goers had earned another respite from the perils of the war; they had braved and escaped the dangers. The ship-goers were entering on another adventure which might be the last, but they were doing it cheerfully and courageously.

What was to be the fate or fortune of these men? Were they to be mined or submarined, to be destroyed or taken prisoners; or were they to come back with a profitable harvest from the sea? The question arose unbidden; but it was beyond the power of man to answer. Here was some of the raw material, not even in uniform, yet taking such a heavy part in the nation's fighting.

These men were everywhere, inside and outside the dock, while crowding nose on to the pontoon were the high-bowed, low-countered steamboats in which they went and caught the fish, and helped to fight the enemy, especially that devil of the deep, the German submarine.

In the old days of the sailing fleets the deadly *coper* was called the "pirate of the North Sea," and the floating grog-shop, with its horrible madness-producing drink, had well earned its title; but that pirate was above-board and could be avoided. There was, however, no escape for the ordinary fishing vessel from the German underwater vessel. Helpless and inoffensive fishing craft, both sail and steam, were repeatedly attacked and destroyed by German torpedoes or guns and the crews killed or drowned, or, what was at times even worse, made prisoners, to be taken to Germany to endure intense suffering.

Many of these little steamboats were still fishing, in certain well defined areas; many of the same sort were sweeping for mines and doing other urgent and important work to enable the British Navy to maintain its strangle-hold on Germany and in conjunction with the Allied navies dominate the seas of the world.

It was inspiring to talk with skippers and men and hear them express their perfect confidence in the Navy and the outcome of the war.

"Oh, no," said one skipper, "the losses aren't much just now—you might almost say there are none hereabouts. Look at this fish. Isn't that a fine show for war-time? And it's mostly North Sea fish, too, for about the last catches have come in from Iceland and the Faroes and that way."

And so it was. These splendid vessels that were all around, and the equally splendid fellows by whom they were manned, had all come in again from the deep sea, from the grounds set apart by the Admiralty for their use, and because of their own consistent courage and their skill and know- ledge they had once more provided a large contribution to the nation's food supply.

At the great fishing-ports, especially Grimsby, Hull, Yarmouth, Aberdeen, Milford Haven and Fleetwood, evidence was given of the country's indebtedness to the toilers of the deep, as such, and those of them who had gone into purely naval service like mine-sweeping and patrolling. At other ports where previously fishermen had been unknown they now assembled as part of the Navy, and in remote bays and estuaries there were formidable fleets of trawlers and drifters which had become units of the nation's fighting forces and were doing invaluable work.

The war necessitated, especially for fishing purposes, vessels that would not in ordinary times have been sent to sea; and disaster sometimes overtook these craft. A case in point was afforded by a Yarmouth shrimper which was lost on July 17, 1917. Three men left early in the morning to go sea-fishing in a small old boat which had been converted into a motor boat. The weather became very rough, and there was little doubt that the men and their craft were lost through foundering in a squall. The tragedy was intensified by the fact that this was the first trip the three men had made in the motor boat.

Old men who had spent their lives at sea, and had won the right to rest ashore, joined the ranks of the fishers and played their part in the war. It was doubtless due to their age that sometimes casualties overtook these superannuated toilers; amongst those who perished being two old fishermen, one aged 75 years and the other 76. They were drowned in September, 1917, in a gale off St. Abbs Head, Berwickshire.

The relative value of fish before and during the war was shown by examples provided at Aberdeen. A few weeks before hostilities began a considerable number of German trawlers were using that port. One of these vessels landed a large quantity of fish. A good part of this was put on the quayside, and at auction fetched only a sovereign. At that time a gigantic halibut was hardly worth the trouble of taking away, and a specimen which would have gladdened the heart of Buckland was in the market, forlorn, and getting high. It was an offence to the senses, and if it had vanished into the water the incident might have been classed as a good riddance. But the case was otherwise indeed at the beginning of the fourth year of war, when it happened that at the market one morning a tine halibut did slip into the water. There was no intention of leaving it there, however. A rare event needed a rare remedy; accordingly a diver was sent down and he recovered the lost treasure, which, being put up for sale, fetched £10 15s. 0d.

Drifters which were herring fishing out of Fleetwood in the summer of 1917 were making very profitable hauls. One catch, landed on a Sunday in August, made £460 at the following day's sale. The boat returned to sea without loss of time and was in again on the Tuesday night, when the catch realised £420. This made a total of £880 for the two catches; an uncommonly good figure, but some of the drifters did even better, one having 90 crans of herrings which averaged £5 a cran, and another 96 crans, which averaged £4 8s. 0d. a cran.

This profitable fishing took place in what might well be considered a safer area than the North Sea; but that region also was well fished. At Scarborough, for example, a fishing-port which had for some reason best known to the Germans received special attention at their hands, there was a fair herring season, and prices were well maintained.

One August day fifty boats arrived with catches of forty crans down. Compared with the pre-war fishings, the landings on the East coast were small, of necessity, but they were a most valuable addition to the nation's food supply. A meagre landing was not due to any fear of German attack or to actual German operations, but was caused by bad weather. The country owed it to the fisherman that it was possible to say, in connection with the fish supply, that prices generally were tolerable. It had to be remembered that in every direction the cost of labour had risen heavily and this naturally affected the price of fish. Prices varied enormously, as they had always done, and from day to day there were astonishing changes, due, often enough, to the vagaries of the weather.

The highest price ever recorded at Scarborough for herrings was reached on September 20, 1917, when £10 18s. 0d. a cran was paid—more than 2½d. each herring, wholesale. Changes came about swiftly in the course of the war; and nowhere more quickly than at sea. The conditions of a given day were altered or obsolete on the morrow of the next. An area which had been open in the North Sea for fishing purposes would be closed, and in carrying out these essential changes the Navy had the prompt and loyal co-operation of the fishermen as a body, though there remained rooted in some of the toilers the conviction that if fish was to be had there was an inherent right to go and get it; and no enemy menace would have deterred some of the skippers and men of fishing vessels. The difficulties of the naval authorities often enough was to save these men from themselves, and police-court proceedings showed with what reckless courage fishermen would enter barred danger-zones. Heavy fines were imposed; but it was only by imprisonment or the threat of it that the disobedience was cured.

Taken altogether, the naval and the fishing forces worked in harmony, showing a striking interdependence. Without the protection of the Navy it would have been impossible for the fishers to work; without the help of the fishers, who had turned sweepers and other trawler ratings, it would have been equally impossible for the Navy to operate successfully. Regulations were in force which had the double purpose of protecting the fisherman and enabling him to carry on his work in the utmost possible security, for his own benefit and the welfare of the nation.

There were in the fourth year of war skippers and men who had been consistently sweeping or patrolling since the war began. For three long years they had done their work in circumstances of peril and discomfort which had never been equalled. Many home ties had been completely severed, and, with something of a dull fatalism, men had settled down to the inevitable.

In the old days of peace, which seemed so visionary, a man had been able to get a look at his home and family once in a long month or so. That was when he sailed from home for the fleet; he was somewhat luckier if he went single-boating, even to Iceland or the White Sea.

But the war changed all that, and the man who had gone off for a six days' trip found himself at the end of six months far from his home and with no prospect of seeing it for many months more. These absences were inevitable, especially when a man happened to be operating in the Mediterranean or any base far from his home.

The fisherman who had been used to the grim, grey North Sea got accustomed to blue Italian skies and waters; but the *Levanter* served as a reminder of the hard gales of the Dogger. On the distant blue waters the mine-sweeping skipper would be smart and trim in his white uniform, while on the greatest and sternest of all the battle-grounds, the North Sea, his blue-clad brother would be carrying on the same perilous and ceaseless work.

A fisherman who had been attached, limpet-like, to the East coast, found himself at some remote Irish, Scotch, Welsh or English base; and, fisher-fashion, he made the best of it. If he pursued his ordinary calling he often decided to change his home, and consequently a skipper would forsake the East coast and, with his wife and children and his goods and chattels, settle on the other side of England.

Wives joined their husbands at naval and fishing bases; and in cases where the husband was in naval employment a woman would cheerfully undertake a twenty-four hours' railway journey, in a crowded third-class compartment, for the sake of spending a few hours or days in his company.

Only those who had made the same journeys, under the same, conditions, fully understood the discomforts of war-time travelling. The trains were fewer in number; they were invariably crowded, largely with liberty men, and to begin such a journey needed a strong bracing effort. But the travellers were indomitably cheerful and friendly; and the skipper's wife found consolation on the return journey by telling of her husband and something—not much—of what he was doing. It was always declared, with pride, that he was "doing his bit" with the best of them.

The multitudes of people who had not been able to see actual drifters and trawlers had an opportunity at the end of the three years of war to look upon cinematograph representations of the vessels and their crews, displays being given in various parts of the country. These productions were Admiralty official films, and they gave decidedly interesting glimpses of such features of the work as could be with discretion shown in public. Some of the preliminary work on shore by men and women was depicted, one picture representing the fitting of a circuit of 144,000 feet of wire. Another picture showed the making of a join in an electric cable, which was commonly called a "pudding."

A very interesting film was that which showed the glass floats used to support submarine-catching nets in the water, and women workers were shown fitting detonators to electrical contact mines. Audiences were also allowed transient views of submergible and floating mines, and drifters were shown containing the war-nets which had superseded the masses or "fleets" of herring nets which had been used in happier and remoter times. A picture was also shown of sweepers actually at sea, carrying out their work under the protection of destroyers; and generally the display gave an instructive, though necessarily very limited, insight into the operations of the mine-sweepers and drifters.

Fishermen had remained singularly unaffected by the industrial turmoil which raged all around them. They had for so long been completely out of touch with the ordinary life and movement of the country that they were almost unacquainted with change or progress in any calling except their own. They were content to go on in more or less the old way, taking inevitable changes philosophically. For the most part they were ignorant of the meaning and aspirations of trades unionism, though in this respect combination had done much to better their general position and to strengthen their hand. But in the immense fishing industry, as in every other industrial direction, the war brought important changes.

As the old order of illiterate smacksman passed, and the new order of smart, well-informed skipper and deep sea toiler took his place, the inevitable unrest arose; a broader view of the situation was taken, the unfairness of many things became obvious, and thoughtful men, while in no way shirking the sufferings and perils of the fishing on the North Sea banks and in remoter waters, developed a vivid realisation of possibilities of improvement.

Looming at the back of the minds of many of the fishermen was the strong hope that time might bring relief in connection with the fleeting system—a system which was bitterly summed up by a smacksman of the old school—"To send a man fleetin's like sendin' him to the gallows."

These vague perceptions took clearer shape as time went on and the war progressed; shadowy ideas were developed into plans of action, and so when the fourth year of war had been entered the men of the deep sea, especially those who were associated with the world's greatest fishing-port, took steps to form a fishing trade union.

A meeting of fishermen, which included many prominent skippers, was held at Grimsby, and this decision was unanimously reached. Rules were framed, and one of the most significant was that no alien skipper should be allowed to command a ship from port, and that only in special circumstances should aliens be allowed in crews.

Time alone would show to what extent this movement would develop, but the momentous step which was taken at the Grimsby meeting was further proof of the fact that when the fishermen set about to do a certain thing they did not do it by halves.

Throughout the war the British fishermen had been one of the special objects of the German naval attacks; but the aim of the Germans was also to sweep as many Allied and neutral fishing vessels off the seas as they could, and they did not hesitate, as time progressed and their own economic situation grew more desperate and hopeless, to apply to neutrals the ruthless methods which they had adopted in connection with their avowed foes.

Wanton attacks, which it was scarcely attempted to justify, were made on inoffensive neutral fishing vessels, and in the fourth year of the war a case was reported in which a Dutch boy, aged fifteen years, was killed by a German submarine which, without warning, torpedoed a Scheveningen herring trawler twenty-five miles from the Dutch coast. After drifting for seven hours a boat containing the ten surviving members of the crew was taken into Ymuiden by another Dutch vessel.

The effect of these ruthless onslaughts was to fill many of the fishermen of neutral countries with dread and to make them determined not to go to sea to carry on their calling. Protests were unavailing, and it was impossible for the injured parties to get redress. If explanations were given by Germany, they took the form of an unavoidable mistake having been made or accusing the injured parties of having brought the losses upon themselves by ignoring or defying the so-called rules which the Germans had imposed on helpless little nations in connection with the war. Almost invariably it was seen that the German "explanation" was directly opposed to the facts which had been stated by survivors of these deliberately-planned outrages on fishing vessels belonging to non-belligerent nations.

Further proof of Germany's cruel and unwarrantable treatment of Dutch fishermen was given by *The Times* special correspondent in Amsterdam. Writing on November 21, 1917, he said it was then certain that five Dutch fishing-boats had been sent to the bottom by the Germans during the last few days. Forty-eight fishermen, the crews of these vessels, returned to Holland from Germany on the previous night. Three of the five fishing-boats were certainly in the area the Germans declared safe for Dutch fishing-boats when they were attacked by a German torpedo-boat and sunk despite all protests.

The Dutchmen were furious at the conduct of their captors, who, they declared, had treated them like beasts. At Wilhelmshaven they were lodged in filthy quarters, which had been previously used for Russian prisoners. Although half-starved, they were unable to eat the rotten potatoes which were given to them as food. They were taken from Wilhelmshaven to Bremen and thence to the frontier, where they were forced to pass a day under wretched conditions.

A significant feature of this outrageous conduct was that amongst the torpedo-boats which sank the Dutch fishing craft was the V 69, which had been badly damaged in the fight with the British in the previous January and had entered Ymuiden, but after being repaired, she was allowed to depart. When she entered the port her wounded were tenderly cared for by the Dutch, who also gave military honours at the burial of her dead; yet her gratitude was shown by sinking Dutch fishing-boats.

When the captain of the V 69 was asked why the Dutch boats were sunk he answered that the Germans feared that the British would employ the fishing vessels to mislead the Germans and destroy them by submarine attacks. The sea, added the captain, must therefore be cleared of them.

★ ★ ★ ★ ★

The story which has been told shows something of what the fishermen did during more than three years of war; how they worked, how they fought, and how they suffered. It is a record, in so far as may be, of their patriotism and heroism, their unflinching loyalty to duty and their constant fight with death.

Amongst so many gallant doings it is hard to choose the bravest; yet there must come to mind the deeds for which the Cross was given to Skipper Watt, the faithfulness of the wireless operator of the *Floandi*, who in the heat of battle was writing up his log when he was claimed by death; and perhaps above them all will loom in solemn grandeur the noble sacrifice of that true patriot and hero. Skipper Thomas Crisp, who, with his dying breath, ordered his confidential books to be thrown into the sea, and, refusing to be a burden to the survivors of his sinking smack, said to his son, "Tom, I'm done. Throw me overboard."

LEONAUR

# ALSO FROM LEONAUR
## AVAILABLE IN SOFTCOVER OR HARDCOVER WITH DUST JACKET

**BOOTS AND SADDLES** *by Elizabeth B. Custer*—The experiences of General Custer's Wife on the Western Plains.

**FANNIE BEERS' CIVIL WAR** *by Fannie A. Beers*—A Confederate Lady's Experiences of Nursing During the Campaigns & Battles of the American Civil War.

**LADY SALE'S AFGHANISTAN** *by Florentia Sale*—An Indomitable Victorian Lady's Account of the Retreat from Kabul During the First Afghan War.

**THE TWO WARS OF MRS DUBERLY** *by Frances Isabella Duberly*—An Intrepid Victorian Lady's Experience of the Crimea and Indian Mutiny.

**LADIES OF WATERLOO** *by Charlotte A. Eaton, Magdalene de Lancey & Juana Smith*—The Experiences of Three Women During the Campaign of 1815: Waterloo Days by Charlotte A. Eaton, A Week at Waterloo by Magdalene de Lancey & Juana's Story by Juana Smith.

**DESPATCH RIDER** *by W. H. L. Watson*—The Experiences of a British Army Motorcycle Despatch Rider During the Opening Battles of the Great War in Europe.

**TWO YEARS BEFORE THE MAST** *by Richard Henry Dana. Jr.*—The account of one young man's experiences serving on board a sailing brig—the Penelope—bound for California, between the years1834-36.

**A SAILOR OF KING GEORGE** *by Frederick Hoffman*—From Midshipman to Captain—Recollections of War at Sea in the Napoleonic Age 1793-1815.

**LORDS OF THE SEA** *by A. T. Mahan*—Great Captains of the Royal Navy During the Age of Sail.

**COGGESHALL'S VOYAGES: VOLUME 1** *by George Coggeshall*—The Recollections of an American Schooner Captain.

**COGGESHALL'S VOYAGES: VOLUME 2** *by George Coggeshall*—The Recollections of an American Schooner Captain.

**TWILIGHT OF EMPIRE** *by Sir Thomas Ussher & Sir George Cockburn*—Two accounts of Napoleon's Journeys in Exile to Elba and St. Helena: Narrative of Events by Sir Thomas Ussher & Napoleon's Last Voyage: Extract of a diary by Sir George Cockburn.

**KIEL AND JUTLAND** *by Georg Von Hase*—The Famous Naval Battle of the First World War from the German Perspective.

LEONAUR

# ALSO FROM LEONAUR

**AVAILABLE IN SOFTCOVER OR HARDCOVER WITH DUST JACKET**

**ESCAPE FROM THE FRENCH** *by Edward Boys*—A Young Royal Navy Midshipman's Adventures During the Napoleonic War.

**THE VOYAGE OF H.M.S. PANDORA** *by Edward Edwards R. N. & George Hamilton, edited by Basil Thomson*—In Pursuit of the Mutineers of the Bounty in the South Seas—1790-1791.

**MEDUSA** *by J. B. Henry Savigny and Alexander Correard and Charlotte Adélaïde Dard* —Narrative of a Voyage to Senegal in 1816 & The Sufferings of the Picard Family After the Shipwreck of the Medusa.

**THE SEA WAR OF 1812 VOLUME 1** *by A. T. Mahan*—A History of the Maritime Conflict.

**THE SEA WAR OF 1812 VOLUME 2** *by A. T. Mahan*—A History of the Maritime Conflict.

**WETHERELL OF H. M. S. HUSSAR** *by John Wetherell*—The Recollections of an Ordinary Seaman of the Royal Navy During the Napoleonic Wars.

**THE NAVAL BRIGADE IN NATAL** *by C. R. N. Burne*—With the Guns of H. M. S. Terrible & H. M. S. Tartar during the Boer War 1899-1900.

**THE VOYAGE OF H. M. S. BOUNTY** *by William Bligh*—The True Story of an 18th Century Voyage of Exploration and Mutiny.

**SHIPWRECK!** *by William Gilly*—The Royal Navy's Disasters at Sea 1793-1849.

**KING'S CUTTERS AND SMUGGLERS: 1700-1855** *by E. Keble Chatterton*—A unique period of maritime history-from the beginning of the eighteenth to the middle of the nineteenth century when British seamen risked all to smuggle valuable goods from wool to tea and spirits from and to the Continent.

**CONFEDERATE BLOCKADE RUNNER** *by John Wilkinson*—The Personal Recollections of an Officer of the Confederate Navy.

**NAVAL BATTLES OF THE NAPOLEONIC WARS** *by W. H. Fitchett*—Cape St. Vincent, the Nile, Cadiz, Copenhagen, Trafalgar & Others.

**PRISONERS OF THE RED DESERT** *by R. S. Gwatkin-Williams*—The Adventures of the Crew of the Tara During the First World War.

**U-BOAT WAR 1914-1918** *by James B. Connolly/Karl von Schenk*—Two Contrasting Accounts from Both Sides of the Conflict at Sea D uring the Great War.

LEONAUR

# ALSO FROM LEONAUR

### AVAILABLE IN SOFTCOVER OR HARDCOVER WITH DUST JACKET

**THE 9TH—THE KING'S (LIVERPOOL REGIMENT) IN THE GREAT WAR 1914 - 1918** *by Enos H. G. Roberts*—Mersey to mud—war and Liverpool men.

**THE GAMBARDIER** *by Mark Severn*—The experiences of a battery of Heavy artillery on the Western Front during the First World War.

**FROM MESSINES TO THIRD YPRES** *by Thomas Floyd*—A personal account of the First World War on the Western front by a 2/5th Lancashire Fusilier.

**THE IRISH GUARDS IN THE GREAT WAR - VOLUME 1** *by Rudyard Kipling*—Edited and Compiled from Their Diaries and Papers—The First Battalion.

**THE IRISH GUARDS IN THE GREAT WAR - VOLUME 1** *by Rudyard Kipling*—Edited and Compiled from Their Diaries and Papers—The Second Battalion.

**ARMOURED CARS IN EDEN** *by K. Roosevelt*—An American President's son serving in Rolls Royce armoured cars with the British in Mesopatamia & with the American Artillery in France during the First World War.

**CHASSEUR OF 1914** *by Marcel Dupont*—Experiences of the twilight of the French Light Cavalry by a young officer during the early battles of the great war in Europe.

**TROOP HORSE & TRENCH** *by R.A. Lloyd*—The experiences of a British Lifeguardsman of the household cavalry fighting on the western front during the First World War 1914-18.

**THE EAST AFRICAN MOUNTED RIFLES** *by C.J. Wilson*—Experiences of the campaign in the East African bush during the First World War.

**THE LONG PATROL** *by George Berrie*—A Novel of Light Horsemen from Gallipoli to the Palestine campaign of the First World War.

**THE FIGHTING CAMELIERS** *by Frank Reid*—The exploits of the Imperial Camel Corps in the desert and Palestine campaigns of the First World War.

**STEEL CHARIOTS IN THE DESERT** *by S. C. Rolls*—The first world war experiences of a Rolls Royce armoured car driver with the Duke of Westminster in Libya and in Arabia with T.E. Lawrence.

**WITH THE IMPERIAL CAMEL CORPS IN THE GREAT WAR** *by Geoffrey Inchbald*—The story of a serving officer with the British 2nd battalion against the Senussi and during the Palestine campaign.

Lightning Source UK Ltd.
Milton Keynes UK
UKHW01f1624210818
327579UK00001BA/13/P